THE NEW
GUIDE TO
GOLF

THE NEW
GUIDE TO
GOLF

CHRIS MEADOWS
WITH
ALLEN F. RICHARDSON

p

This is a Parragon Publishing Book

Copyright © Parragon 2001

Parragon Publishing
Queen Street House
4 Queen Street
Bath BA1 1HE
United Kingdom

Designed, produced and packaged by
Stonecastle Graphics Limited

Edited by Philip de Ste. Croix

ISBN 0-75255-132-9

Printed in Italy

Photography by Bill Johnston

Film kindly supplied by Fuji

I would like to thank The Wisley Golf Club,
Surrey, England and Le Prince de Provence,
Vidauban, France for allowing me the use of
their wonderful golfing facilities. They are
truly two of the finest golf courses to be
found anywhere in Europe.

Thanks also go to my professional colleague
Daniel Belcher, Nicola Bustin, my wife
Kayo, to the two men who worked so
closely with me in over a year of preparation,
Allen Richardson and Bill Johnston, but
most of all to my teacher Ian Connelly who
developed my love for golf and gave me the
passion to teach this great game.

CONTENTS

◆ ◆ ◆ ◆ ◆

A VOYAGE OF DISCOVERY

◆ ◆ ◆ ◆ ◆

CHRIS MEADOWS' love of the game began at the age of 12. While caddying at a golf club in North London, he was introduced to a Scottish professional, Ian Connelly. In the mid 1970s Connelly was coaching the cream of European talent including his star pupil Nick Faldo. Meadows, himself aspiring to become a successful tour player, found himself intrigued by the array of skills Connelly possessed and the way he developed players' minds and movements, often taking them from nothing to scratch golfers. By the age of 16 Chris knew that he had begun a voyage of discovery that would last a lifetime.

Over an eight-year period working with Connelly as both pupil and teacher, Meadows spent literally thousands of hours watching players of all standards being taught by Connelly on practice grounds across Europe. By now he'd begun using his own game as a testbed, seeking to understand the perfect motion. His golf was improving to a high standard, but he found that his own stable of players were demanding more and more of his time.

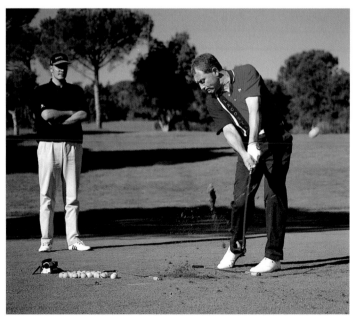

THE RIGHT ENVIRONMENT

Although commanding his own head pro position by the age of 21, increasingly Meadows became frustrated with the generally poor teaching conditions in the UK. He vowed to develop his own school of excellence where golfers of all standards could be stimulated by their environment, as well as by their teacher. In 1987 Meadows acquired The Regent's Park Golf & Tennis School in the heart of Central London. Driven by the belief that seeing is believing, he installed the most advanced video systems of the time so that students of the school could understand and see for themselves their own swing in action. The school soon became an outstanding success

Left: A stimulating environment is an essential part of learning. Meadows designs all his golf schools with a strong emphasis on visual learning. He says 'A picture is worth a thousand words and that's why video analysis and mirrors are so useful to both pupil and teacher.'

and Meadows was invited to write instructional columns for numerous golf publications. He developed the concept for *Improve your Golf* (a golf learning manual) that was published in the UK, Australasia, Canada and even translated into Japanese selling over 500,000 copies in total. He has written five instructional golf books, appeared on UK television on BBC, Channel 4, Channel 5 and many satellite channels and has made four instructional videos.

In 1997 Meadows opened the first Metro Golf Centre in London. These are centers of golfing excellence incorporating everything a golfer might ever need to advance their game. Based on a golf-for-all philosophy, the center has become the industry standard for golf centers in Europe.

Above: If it's fun, you'll keep at it – enjoy your 'voyage of discovery.'

www.chrismeadowsgolf.com

Meadows has always used his entrepreneurial skills to take the game to the people and he has recently launched an interactive website 'www.chrismeadowsgolf.com.' The site is a very different experience in learning. Driven once again by visual aids, simplicity and structure (the trademark of Meadows teaching), it helps players plan their improvement and effectively guides them to their chosen objective.

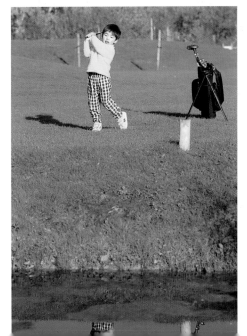

Left: If your children want to play the game, put them in a group class first – they'll have fun and meet friends with whom they can play.

INTRODUCTION

◆ ▪ ▪ ▪ ◆

*Offering so many challenges in
so many different environments
in the company of so many
friends — the game of golf is
truly a game for life.*

INTRODUCTION

◆ ◆ ◆ ◆ ◆

Golfers are dreamers and seekers.
From the first time we pick up a club and hit that small, round object
known as a golf ball toward the sky, we are part of a tradition that
stretches back through generations of time, linking us to an ancient
shepherd who first struck a rock with a stick along the coastal grassland
of Scotland.

FROM THAT moment we often embark on a life-long quest to improve how we play the game – a game that for most of us eventually becomes both a love and an obsession. From tour pro to club champion to rank beginner, we constantly tinker with our swings, adjust our grips and stances, and try to plant an endless series of 'swing thoughts' in our brains.

The hope is that by tomorrow, next weekend – or at least the end of the year – we will finally play a miracle round.

GOLFING DREAMS

The form that round takes will vary. We might dream of breaking 100 or 70, sinking an eagle putt, winning the club championship, or standing on the 18th tee with a chance to seize the Open. But at the very least, we all yearn for the day when we'll win that side bet struck with our similarly devoted friends, while savoring a drink at the 19th hole. Then we'll enjoy the afterglow of a memorable day, with everyone mentally replaying their rounds, and generously

The hours spent working on my game have been some of the most enjoyable of my life. I hope this book also makes learning fun for you in your quest to improve your game.

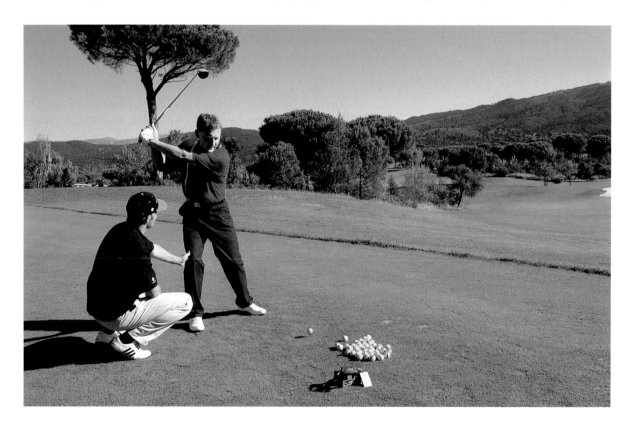

reviewing each other's remembered highlights.

But even when we are not playing the game, we take lessons, analyze how more gifted players perform on television, and read countless articles about the the latest technology in club design, swing theory, and putting technique.

I know. I've spent a lifetime playing, teaching and trying to improve my own game – and this book is the product of my quest, while your purchase of it is undoubtedly proof that you share my passion.

But now it's time to simplify things.

The New Guide to Golf is structured around a single, essential idea: instead of worrying about all the things you need to know, this book will allow you to focus on the essentials that you cannot do without.

I have structured this book so that anyone – from a complete beginner to an advanced player – can either dip into it for specific advice, or simply enjoy reading it from cover to cover. I've started with the basic fundamentals of the movement. Looking first at set-up and then moving on to the backswing and throughswing. If you are going to realize your true potential then these areas of your golf swing have to be developed correctly. Taking short cuts here will only lead to greater problems later on. I then move on to the short game – chipping, pitching, bunker play, and putting. Once again there are fundamental techniques that you will need to master in these areas of the game before you can move on. Given that over 50 per cent of your shots will be played from within twenty yards (18m) of the green, time spent on this section of the game will prove to be very worthwhile.

LEARNING IN THE RIGHT ORDER

I also include advice on how to practice. Practice is truly the 'mother of skill' and it is only by applying what you learn on these pages that you will be able to both develop and transform your game. Whether you are new to the game or have been playing for

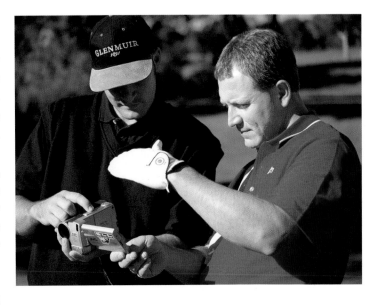

years, be patient. Nobody has ever become a fine player in a matter of a few months. The more I have played and taught this great game, the more I have realized that one has to work in order. So begin with the set-up, practice it, understand it, feel comfortable with it, and then move on to the backswing. Then move to the throughswing, and so on. In this way your mind and body will absorb the information and your confidence will begin to grow.

Improvement is a journey – so let's embark on it together and have fun along the way.

Over the years I have had the opportunity to work with some great teachers who have shared their knowledge with me. It is now my privilege to share my knowledge with you.

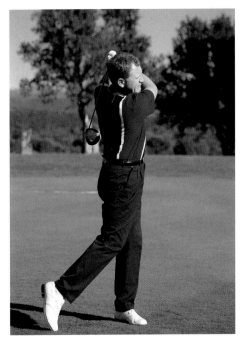

The great thing about golf is we are always learning. When man has mastered the wildest dreams of future technology, he will still be working on his golf swing!

PREPARATION

◆◆◆◆◆

A golf swing takes around one second to perform. Therefore, the position you assume at the set-up is critical – it will either enable or disable your golf swing from the word 'go.'

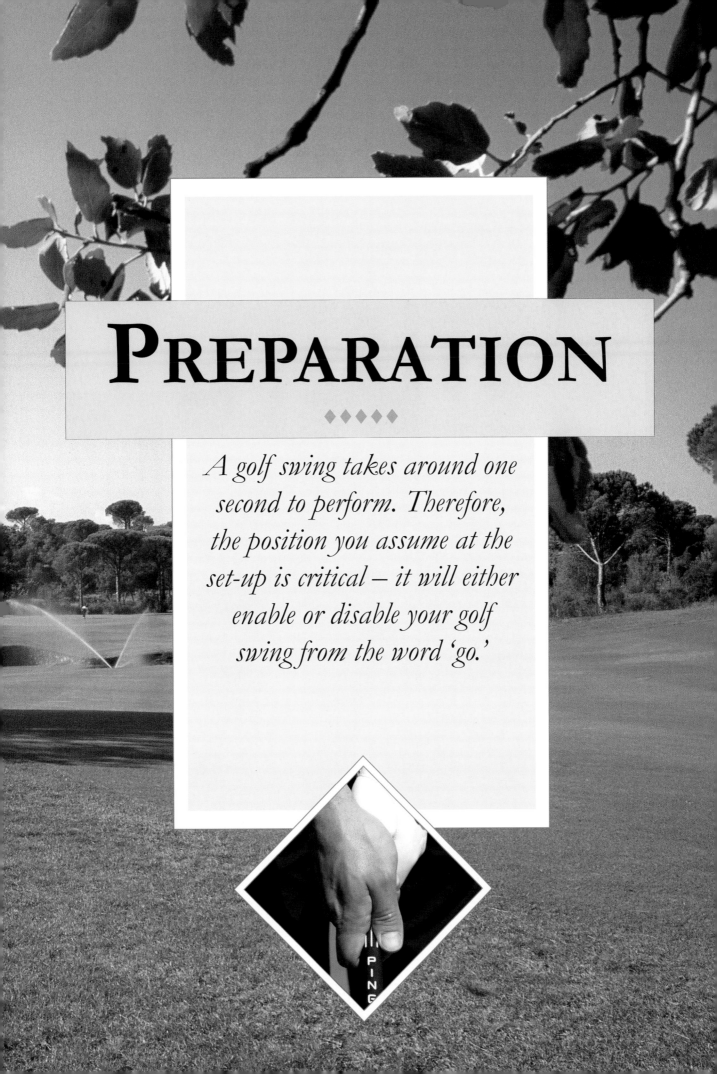

PREPARATION – GOLF'S FUNDAMENTALS

◆◆◆◆◆

At one time it was fashionable to think of golfers as anything but athletic. After all, golf – even at the highest level – is played at a leisurely pace by men and women of all ages, and, in some cases, by children. Endurance is hardly a necessity, and no running, jumping, or heavy lifting is required.

IN FACT, it seemed that to play the game in a mere three to four hours, all one had to do was walk a few miles – or in some cases, not even that. Many courses (especially in America) provide – or even require – golfers to use a motorized cart or have a caddy to carry one's bag.

But watching a slow-motion video of golfers from the legendary Ben Hogan to current superstars such as Tiger Woods and Lee Westwood proves conclusively otherwise. Swinging a golf club in the correct way involves a series of finely tuned and very athletic moves, none of which is possible without the right set-up.

Mastering such fundamentals as the correct stance, posture, and grip makes all the difference once a golfer finally lets it rip, leading either to a pure, clean hit – or any number of golfing disasters.

Gripping the club

Once you've aimed the clubhead, apply the hands to the club. For the right hander, always begin with your left hand followed by the right.

Begin by placing the club across the middle joint of the index finger of your left hand and under the palm pad of your hand. The left hand thumb should fall sightly right of center on the club. Ensure the back of your left hand and the palm of your right hand point at the target.

THE GRIP

Most golfers think that the grip is one of the least glamorous aspects of the golf swing. But assuming the proper grip can be a thing of beauty – look at how athletic and powerful the grips of many professionals appear next time you watch a tournament. And forming a proper grip is certainly the essential starting point to playing that dream round.

Think of it this way. If the clubhead is the only object that comes into direct contact with the ball, the grip is the only part of a golfer's anatomy that makes contact with the club. In other words, a golfer uses the grip to transfer any power and skill he or she might possess to the object that propels the ball toward the hole. Have I got your attention now?

FORMING A PROPER GRIP

Here's how to assume a correct grip.

It has often been said that no two grips – like individual swings – are exactly alike, and I would find it hard to disagree with that statement. However, there are certain basics I can recommend. Once you understand and master those, you can adjust and experiment with your grip until it is comfortable and suits your swing.

But first a quick word of warning here. Forming the proper grip can take weeks, if not months, of practice before doing so becomes second nature to you. The golf grip is not a particularly natural positioning of the hands.

So I would suggest that dedicated golfers keep a club handy and practice taking their grip while watching television or, if possible, even while working in the office. And if you are in the process of changing your grip, I would caution you not to hit golf shots for as long as it takes to become comfortable with that change.

POSITIONING THE LEFT HAND

Allow your arms to hang naturally by your sides and then rest the sole of a club on the ground. Now place the grip of the club in the left hand leaving the top half-inch

A union of two hands

(1.3cm) of the club protruding from the top of your hand.

Position the club so that it runs diagonally from the middle joint of your index finger to the bottom joint of your little finger, then rest the club against the fleshy pad at the bottom of your hand. Finally, wrap your fingers around, with your thumb falling slightly to the right of center down the shaft.

Now take a look at what you've done. You should be able to see two knuckles on the back of your hand, and a 'V' – formed by the line between the first joint of the index finger and the thumb – pointing toward your right ear or shoulder.

Now place your right hand on the golf club, positioning your club in the two center fingers of your hand. It is essential that your club is held in your fingers and not in the palm of your hand. Your little finger should sit in the cleft between the index and middle finger of your left hand.

Positioning the right hand

Now close your right hand over your left thumb so that it's covered by your right hand. The thumb and forefinger of your right hand should touch or almost touch.

THE RIGHT HAND IN THE GRIP

◆ ◆ ◆ ◆ ◆

It's time to add the right hand to your grip. But before you do, let me introduce a word of caution, especially if you are right-handed. Make sure the right hand does not try to take over the grip and dominate your left hand.

THE GOLF grip is different from many other things we do in life with our hands. In the case of the golf grip, both hands must work together, rather than separately. Think of it as shaking hands with yourself or as clapping. You want each hand to be an equal partner, working together so you can swing the golf club better.

By the way, when the complete grip is assumed, the image of clapping becomes even more appropriate. A good grip means

The natural position of the hands

A good grip will always ensure that the back of your left hand and palm of your right hand face the target.

essentially that both palms face each other, while the back of the left hand faces the target, and the palm of the right hand also faces the target.

ADDING THE RIGHT HAND

The right hand can be joined to the left in the grip in three different ways, depending on the position of the last or little finger. The three basic golf grips are:

• The traditional overlapping, or Vardon, grip where the little finger sits in the cleft between the index and ring finger of your left hand. (The Vardon grip, as you may know, was popularized by the legendary British golfer Harry Vardon.)

• The interlocking, where the right little finger lies between the first two fingers of your left hand and the left index finger is extended over the back of the right hand.

• The ten-finger or baseball grip, where each hand grips the club separately – the base of the right touching the top of the left – but with the fingers independent of each other.

Most golfers, pro and amateur alike, favor the Vardon grip for both feel and the effortless way it links the hands together as a unit. It can seem strange initially, however, and it takes getting used to for the beginner.

The interlocking grip is useful for golfers with smaller hands. Jack Nicklaus uses the interlock. The baseball grip is ideal for children and those with weak hands, although a former pro named Art Wall used it and was famous for hitting holes-in-one.

The three grips

Interlocking grip.

Overlapping grip.

Baseball grip.

Above: The three basic types of grip.

THE FINAL STAGE

Assuming the final stage of the grip is easy. Essentially, the right hand holds the club shaft in the fingers – never let it ride up into the palm. First, position the little finger of your right hand in the cleft between your left forefinger and middle finger, then wrap the rest of the fingers of your right hand around the club along the bottom joint, folding over your hand by fitting the vertical crease in your palm around the left thumb.

Meanwhile, your right thumb runs diagonally across the top, the tip resting near or lightly against the first finger of your right hand. The 'V' formed between the thumb and forefinger of your right hand should point between the right shoulder and chin.

GRIP PRESSURE

A final word about the grip. One of the most common faults of beginners is applying too much pressure with their hands, squeezing the club in a death grip. They often think that the harder they squeeze, the harder they'll hit the ball. Instead, it will guarantee a bad shot.

For years, golf instructors have searched for the appropriate analogy on how tightly – or not – to hold a club, suggesting that one should not grip a club any tighter than a fountain pen, an open tube of toothpaste, or a small, fragile bird.

NATURAL HOLD

My recommendation is simply to hold the club naturally, meaning not too tightly and not too loosely. Think again about the athleticism of golf. Your grip should be firm enough to ensure that the club does not slip out of your hands, or that your fingers do not come partially off the shaft at the top of the backswing or during the follow-through.

Passive right side

When placing your right hand on the golf club, ensure that your right shoulder is lower than your left shoulder. This will help establish your head and body in the correct position at the completed set-up.

But your grip should also be supple enough not to make you tense up, especially through the forearms. Any tension in the hands, arms and/or shoulders will destroy your ability to swing the club with the sort of fluid grace you see the best golfers use.

In other words, you want to exert only the amount of grip pressure that will let you swing like an athlete.

GRIPPING HONORS

Harry Vardon did not invent the popular grip that still bears his name. That honor goes to Johnny Laidlay, the British Amateur champion in 1889 and 1891. But because Vardon was the most famous golfer of his time – winning a record six Open Championships from 1896-1914 – golfers everywhere sought to emulate him when he adopted Laidlay's innovation.

THE SET-UP

◆ ◆ ◆ ◆ ◆

*Positioning the body in relation to the ball and target is known as the
set-up, or stance – and the key word here is balance. All athletic
movement takes place from a balanced starting position.*

THINK OF a footballer preparing to take a penalty or a baseball player taking his stance at the plate. The one thing they have in common is that their feet are positioned on the ground in a dynamic way that will allow them to shift their weight and use their body to propel a ball toward their target. Just like the golf swing.

PARALLEL RELATIONSHIPS

So where do we start in any discussion of the set-up? How about from the ground up. One of the unique things about golf is that we set our body up in a parallel relationship to an imaginary line that runs to our target.

In golf, we usually refer to that relationship as being square to the target, and we can visualize the set-up position along a set of railroad tracks, with the golfer parallel to one rail, and the clubhead, ball, and target line along the opposite rail. In the distance, both rails converge like lines of perspective at the target.

Any deviation from this parallel relationship will result in an attempt to correct any number of resultant problems during the swing, which eventually produces a swing fault. This could result in a loss of distance or directional accuracy.

But we'll cover that in more detail in 'Pre-Shot Routine,' where we learn how to aim, set-up, and swing down those imaginary tracks toward a spot on the fairway or to the flagstick.

GOOD BODY ANGLES

Everything the golfer does in his or her set-up must conform to the goal of taking a stance in direct relation to where the ball will eventually fly – what the famous golf guru

David Leadbetter likes to call setting up good, level body angles. Of course, setting up any body angle starts with the feet.

For decades, golf instructors have debated the position of the feet in relationship to this line. Some, such as Ben Hogan, favored having the back foot straight, or perpendicular, to the line of

Get in position to swing

The foundation of a good golf swing begins with the set-up. The time you spend developing good balance and position will make building your golf swing much easier.

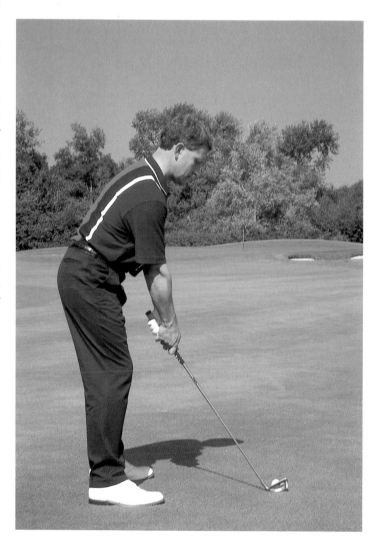

flight, and the front foot angled out toward the target by about 20 to 30 degrees. This works for many tour professionals, but it also tends to shorten or restrict the turn of many less experienced golfers.

NATURAL POSITIONING

I prefer the approach whereby the feet are placed in the most natural, or athletic, position. In other words, both feet should be lined up with that imaginary railroad track, but turned out slightly – again about 20 to 30 degrees – in relation to one another. Picture a clock with the ball at high noon. Your left foot should point to around 11 o'clock, while your right foot would aim at 1 o'clock.

This promotes the most balanced and natural position in which to anchor our set-up, giving our stance what Leadbetter calls 'dynamic balance.' Although it may seem an obvious point, remember that the feet are your only contact with Mother Earth while you swing the golf club. Positioning them correctly is the key to prevent you from swaying off the ball, or even coming close to toppling over as you bring the clubhead around your body at over 100mph (160km/h).

In other words, losing your balance means losing it. Period!

WEIGHT DISTRIBUTION

One key to balance in the set-up is an even distribution of weight between the left and right foot. Unless you are hitting a short pitch or chip, you should not favor either foot in your set-up.

Alignment of the clubhead and body

Left: Begin by positioning the club so that the leading edge is at right angles to the ball-to-target line. Then align your feet, hips, and shoulders so that they are positioned parallel to your ball-to-target line. During practice it's a good idea to put two clubs on the ground as shown parallel to your ball-to-target line.

Below: A club placed at right angles to the clubs indicating the ball-to-target line will help you to visualize your ball position.

Ball position

Position of feet

Left: Turning your feet out as shown will help with maintaining your balance and assist your follow-through.

THE BALANCED SET-UP

◆◆◆◆◆

The width of your stance and where you position the golf ball in relation to your feet are important ingredients of a proper set-up. Almost everyone who has ever swung a golf club knows that one of the standard rules dictates that a golfer should position his or her feet roughly shoulder-width apart.

BUT WHAT many golfers forget – or don't ever realize – is this means shoulder-width as measured from the inside of the heels, rather than the outside of the feet. The width will also vary slightly according to which club is used, from the driver down to the sand wedge.

The shoulder-width rule begins with a standard 5-iron set-up. In this position, two parallel lines drawn from the outside of the shoulders would end at the inside of the heels. Widen the width a few inches for the longer irons and woods, and narrow it for the shorter irons.

TRADITIONAL ARGUMENTS

That brings us to ball position, which raises another time-honored argument among dozens of so-called golf gurus. For years Jack Nicklaus advocated putting the ball on a line just inside the left heel for all shots, while others have insisted that the distance

of the ball from the front foot should vary, depending on the length of the club used.

I've seen both methods work well, so I would suggest experimenting with each variation until you find the one that works best for your game. Start with the ball opposite the instep of your front foot for the driver, then move the ball back by a quarter inch (0.65cm) or so as you use progressively shorter clubs until you get to the wedges, when the ball should be roughly in the middle of the stance. Or, like Nicklaus, try to hit every club off the left heel.

Of course, depending on whether we want to work the ball low under the wind, or high over an intervening tree, that rule will vary.

POWER AND CONTROL

Now it is time to move from the feet to the body, since keeping our feet in the right place is only part of the story, no matter how vital it is.

Short iron.

Medium iron.

Long iron.

The three positions above show how to position your golf ball. Center for short irons, middle for medium irons, and inside of left heel for long irons and woods.

Experiment by placing the ball just inside your left heel for all shots – see what works and stick to it.

Wood.

Balancing the swing

Left and above: The width of your stance increases as your club gets longer. As a rule of thumb, with a medium iron the outside of your heels should be at shoulder-width, whereas with your wood, the inside of your heels should be at shoulder-width.

The set-up should be natural and athletic. That means balancing the rest of the body frame over the feet in a way that keeps the golfer stable and yet ready to perform the complex and athletic movement of the golf swing. This is how you bring power and control to your game, and create a repeating swing that will not only help you strike the ball both well and consistently, but give you a swing that will hold up under pressure.

In explaining how this works, I like to borrow an image created by another famous golf guru, Jimmy Ballard, in his book. Ballard asked his readers to imagine him standing on a platform, holding a large golf bag that weighed a great deal, with someone below ready to catch that load in his hands.

How would the recipient position himself do this?

BRACE YOURSELF

Obviously, as Ballard explained, anyone in such a position would instinctively spread their feet to about shoulder-width and brace themselves. With the feet well-grounded, and the body weight spread from the balls to the heels of each foot, they would also tend to flex their knees – like a boxer ready to receive or deliver a blow.

In addition, the posterior would naturally jut out slightly to straighten the spine, keeping the back erect. Meanwhile, the upper arms would be tucked into the sides of the chest to brace the upper torso.

In other words, the larger muscles of the legs, chest, and shoulders would be angled and tied in toward the center of the body like the supports of a bridge, and the person would be ready to catch that imaginary bag.

AGILITY AND STRENGTH

I like this image for what it teaches us about balance, agility, and strength. But I want to stress a further point. Later we will add the actual golf swing to our set-up. So for now, don't get hung up on the idea of simply bracing to catch a heavy load someone might be throwing down to you!

The idea is to create a stance that is athletic, but not one that promotes any restriction or rigidity. In order to repeat a golf swing, it needs a firm, but flexible, foundation.

Above: Turning your body will soon show whether you are balanced, even without a golf club.

Above: Practice turning to a coiled position and assessing the foundation of your swing.

POWER POSTURE IN THE SET-UP

◆ ◆ ◆ ◆ ◆

The correct posture is the final ingredient that will help your set-up support the golf swing. In fact, posture can dictate how well a golfer swings his or her club. Standing too erect inhibits the shoulder turn and the free movement of the arms, while crouching too much forces the arms to lift up, often resulting in poor contact with the ball.

TAKE A 5-iron, assume a good grip, and hold the club out from the waist at about a 45 degree angle. Stand straight up – while remaining supple and at ease – then bend from the hips – not the waist! As you do, your rear end should jut out slightly into a semi-sitting position and your back, or spine, angle should stay straight.

SWING RADIUS

Finally, flex your knees slightly and ground the club, letting your arms hang naturally from your upper body, with your left arm forming an almost straight line from the top of the shoulder to the clubhead.

This line, by the way, will constitute the radius of your swing and you must strive to maintain it as a constant throughout that

Establishing good posture

To establish your posture, simply bend forward from your hips keeping your head up. Now sit back and flex your legs slightly at the knee in order to counterbalance the bend forward. Your weight should end up slightly backward of center.

MODEL SET-UPS

Next time you watch the pros on television, study their set-up position, trying to find the golfer closest to you in size. If you are tall, I would recommend focusing on Ernie Els or Nick Faldo, while shorter players would do well to emulate Ian Woosnam or Gary Player.

swing, which we will discuss further in sections to come.

If you have done all of the above correctly, your weight should feel balanced from the balls of your feet to the heels, and overall, you should feel comfortable, centered, and yet dynamically positioned, in what David Leadbetter calls the 'sit-tall' position.

Now your set-up includes the correct posture and you can create the axis from which a powerful and controlled swing can be executed.

TRIANGLE AND STEEPLE

One final note on the set-up. With the left arm straight and the right arm also fully extended – but slightly relaxed – you should feel some pressure under the armpits or up around the highest reaches of your chest.

Later, we will see how this triangle – formed by the arms and chest – is tied together and functions in the swing as you begin your turn. Ben Hogan called this a triangle with the club emerging like the 'spire of a steeple.' That's not a bad image for something as beautiful as a well-executed golf swing.

Connection

Above: Your upper arms should feel a light connection with your chest.

Position of weight

Above: With your posture complete, check that your weight is slightly backward of center.

Create space

When you sit back in your posture you create space for your golf club and achieve good balance.

Above: To sense just how your lower body should feel at set-up, throw something heavy up in the air and catch it. You will instinctively flex in the same way as you should at address.

THE PRE-SHOT ROUTINE

◆◆◆◆◆

Consistency is the key to golf. Having a reliable, repeating swing helps the golfer hit fairways and greens in the regulation number of shots. But when a shot is less than perfect, being able to get up and down from bunkers and off the fringe of greens is essential. Once on the green, a solid putting stroke is vital to avoiding three-putts – these are all aided by a pre-shot routine.

IF YOU can add all of the above qualities together, you will have a consistent game, which leads to lower scores and winning golf.

So why not incorporate that idea into the very act of stepping up to the ball, before taking each shot and putt? At the very least, you'll develop a pre-shot routine that helps you concentrate and deal with tension. At the very best, I can guarantee you will play better golf overall.

COMMON TRAITS

How can I offer such solid assurance? Because with a pre-shot routine, you have already played the shot in your mind, and having done so, you will know which club to select, how to hit it, and where. Watch the pros. If they have one thing in common, it is that their pre-shot routine never varies, from shot to shot, from day to day – and often throughout their entire careers.

Consistency.

I can't say it enough. It's the key to golf. So develop your own pre-shot routine, and give yourself something to fall back on – something you can always rely on. It's the one weapon in your bag that should never vary.

VISUALIZING THE SHOT

The pre-shot routine is a blend of the physical skills you have now learned in 'Preparation' – including the proper posture, alignment, and set-up or stance – and certain mental skills that will help you hit the ball to your intended target.

The latter concept is called 'visualization,' a method of seeing not only where you want

Always be sure where you are aiming – choose your target.

Place your clubhead down so that the leading edge of the golf club is at right angles to the ball-to-target line.

Then position your feet, hips and shoulders so that they are parallel to your ball-to-target line.

PREPARATION 25

the ball to go, but how you will get it there. Most beginners find visualization difficult. But that will improve with experience, especially after a golfer accumulates a mental gallery of good shots that he or she can call upon when confronted by a variety of situations. Some aspects of golf do get easier with time, and this is one area that is proof of that, as anyone who has played the game for more than a few years can attest.

You still may not be able to execute the shot perfectly every time, but you will at least know how to picture a good outcome, and that helps give you the confidence to approach each shot correctly.

CONFIDENT APPROACH

Obviously, positive thinking is a prerequisite here, especially if the shot you are trying to visualize is a tough one – say over a bunker or out of the rough. But at the same time, be realistic. It makes no sense conjuring up the image of a miracle strike – even if you have pulled a few off in the past – or a shot you simply are not capable of hitting. Even when visualizing, you should play within yourself.

MENTAL IMAGES

The pre-shot routine should start as soon as you walk on to the tee or when you reach your ball on the fairway.

First, try to gauge the difficulty of the shot by studying what lies before you on the course and assessing what the conditions are. Then decide on the type of stroke you want to play and how you will shape the flight of the ball.

Finally, see the shot in your mind, from the moment it leaves the clubhead until it reaches the ground – even down to mentally watching it roll up the fairway or toward the pin on the green.

Below: Visualization of just what you want to do with your shot is crucial. Seeing your shot in your mind will tell your body what you want it to do. Only once you have a clear image in your mind should you attempt to play your shot.

A closer target can help your alignment. Choose a piece of grass, or a leaf, lying on your ball-to-target line no more than six inches in front of the golf club.

Once your club and body are in line, place your left hand in position.

Now place the right hand on the golf club – remember to lower your right shoulder when doing this.

THE BACKSWING

◆◆◆◆◆

Like a sprinter leaving the blocks, a smooth, fluid beginning to the backswing is the key to a powerful, genuinely athletic swing.

THE BACKSWING

◆ ◆ ◆ ◆ ◆

It is always hard to make the first move. I don't have to tell you about the many situations in life where that axiom applies. But it is also a key in any sporting activity – and especially in the golf swing. Like a sprinter about to explode from the blocks, you have to be both poised and ready to go, but also relaxed enough to unleash your full power smoothly.

IN THE previous section, I explained how to assume a solid grip, a balanced and dynamic set-up – or stance – and a pre-shot routine that can help ease tension and serve as a mini-rehearsal for the real thing.

But now it really is time for the real thing. The first move in the golf swing – what is termed the backswing. Get this part right, and you have built the foundation for a powerful, athletic swing. But get it wrong, and nothing good can follow. The backswing is the key to the swing itself – which in turn is the central action of golf.

PROGRAM YOUR BODY

So how should you approach the first move?

I believe you must fully understand what your body will be doing in the backswing, then program it accordingly through hours of practice. Initially, much of this practice will not involve hitting any golf balls. Simply picking up a club and heading for the driving range is a recipe for disaster.

So, don't go near a golf ball…at least for now. If you are a beginner and want to learn how to swing the club properly, this is the best advice I can give you. And if you are an experienced player – but have had limited success – it's even better advice.

MASTER THE BODY

You must first understand the role of your body in the swing – and please note that I said the body, rather than specifically mentioning the role of the hands, wrists, and arms. Most golfers concentrate on the latter,

The first move in the golf swing is the most important part of it. A low, slow takeaway will help ensure that your arms, hands, and body move in one coordinated movement.

The first move

DON'T FREEZE UP

Once you have gone through your pre-shot routine and assumed your stance, don't stop – as so many golfers do – by grounding the club behind the ball and going into a trance that leads to muscle tension. Pull the trigger as quickly – yet smoothly – as possible.

Exercise 1

Exercise 2

rather than the former, whether consciously or not. Unless you also fully comprehend the role of the large muscles of the upper torso, hips, and legs in the golf swing, and how they work together with the arms, hands, and shoulders – you'll never learn or master a proper swing.

But if you do understand this physical combination, I can promise you'll begin executing the first move in a way that will put you in the correct position at the top of the backswing. In turn, that will allow you to start the downswing – or what I prefer to call the throughswing – in the most efficient and powerful way possible.

The end result? You will propel the ball toward its intended target with both accuracy and length, setting up the possibility of a good score. But again, if you have not mastered the basic technique, the first move will cause you problems and lead to any number of golfing disasters

Left: In order to teach your arms and body to move together, try placing a credit card between your left arm and ribs. The right arm should not be held as tightly to the body, so a head cover should be placed under your right armpit.

Right: Ensure that when you initiate your takeaway, you rotate your body immediately.

The takeaway

DEVELOPING A REPEATABLE SWING

◆ ◆ ◆ ◆ ◆

You may know the feeling: You are standing on the first tee, and your playing partners are waiting for you…other people may also be standing nearby, watching and waiting as well, eager for you to get off so they can start their rounds…

AT SUCH times, it's very easy to get tense and even freeze over the ball, especially if you lack confidence in how to make that first move. If this happens, you are in big trouble. Add a faulty technique to the mix, and you'll really wish you had stayed at home.

THE REPEATABLE SWING

Here's how to avoid that nightmare scenario and hit a great shot – over and over and over again. By making the correct first move, you will prepare yourself for what's called the 'repeatable' (as in reliable) swing.

Once you have mastered this basic movement, you are well on your way to that goal, because the repeatable swing is just that – repeatable. It will not break down when you are tired, nervous, or under pressure. You'll play better overall – and if your temperament is right – you'll even start winning competitions.

Now that dream round is closer to reality, but only if you can make the first move properly.

THE BASIC SWING

Let me pause here for just one moment, and add a note about how this section and the following one will be structured.

Of course, the swing is one continuous, athletic movement. But in order to understand best how it works – and how you

can make it work for you – my approach will consist of examining the swing in two parts, breaking down each element of the backswing and throughswing, until you thoroughly understand each.

Then we'll put it all together and study the finished product – a swing that you can take to the course. A swing that you can start working on that will eventually produce consistently lower scores.

GOLFING SECRETS

Learning the proper swing is the only way to unlock the basic secrets of golf – which is equally true both for the beginner and the professional. Yes, even the pros are constantly learning about the swing, and re-tooling their basic movement. Some of the recent changes in the approach of Tiger Woods and Phil Mickelson bear out the truth of this.

In some cases, a few pros have even scrapped a successful swing and completely revamped their basic motion. Nick Faldo is the most famous example of that. Along with golf guru David Leadbetter, Faldo completely remodeled his swing, using many of the basic ideas and techniques that I am about to describe in this section.

The result, as we all know, was a better swing under pressure and increased success on the golf course.

You can do the same.

The repeatable swing

A repeatable golf swing is the result of a good set-up combined with a smooth, unhurried rotation of the body with the arms forming a wide arc throughout the back- and throughswings. Practiced regularly, this will become a consistent movement.

STARTING FROM SCRATCH

In the early 80s, Faldo was the top-ranked golfer in Europe. But Faldo knew his swing hid a multitude of faults that wouldn't stand up under the pressure of the world's 'major' tournaments. So he approached British coach David Leadbetter, who told him the refit would mean almost completely scrapping his swing, a process that could take at least two years – during which his game, and his earnings, would suffer. But Faldo was determined to become one of the world's best golfers, so he plunged into the task with relish, often practicing such long hours that his hands bled. Faldo failed to win any tournaments in 1985-86. But in 1987, as he finally became more comfortable with his re-tooled swing, the discipline began to pay off. After capturing the Spanish Open, Faldo snatched his first 'major' triumph, coming from three behind at Muirfield to defeat American Paul Azinger for the British Open Championship. In the years since, Faldo has won a host of tournaments in both Europe and the USA, plus several additional majors, including two more Opens and three US Masters to rank him among the greatest golfers of his time

THE CONNECTED SWING

◆ ◆ ◆ ◆ ◆

Tee up the ball, take your grip, assume your stance, and go through a pre-shot routine. Now you are ready for that first move into the backswing.

TO START with, you want to conjure up a feeling of lightness throughout your body, but especially in your hands, arms, shoulders, and upper torso. At the same time, you want your legs to be poised and stable – but never rigid – evenly distributing your weight in order to support a dynamic movement away from the ball.

Next, you want to think about making that first move with a nice feeling of rhythm and tempo, easing into the backswing in a way that builds toward a consistent, overall swing, and ultimately the release of maximum power into the ball.

Finally, you want to tie all of the above sensations together in what I like to call the 'connected' swing.

FEELING CONNECTED

Your hands, arms, shoulders, and upper torso should move together, turning back and coiling behind the ball – partly in opposition to the lesser turn of the hips (more on that later) – while they are anchored by the stable foundation provided by the legs.

This feeling of connection is the secret to building a consistent, athletic golf swing that will repeat time after time – and, most importantly, under pressure.

By tying in the hands and arms with the larger muscles of the upper body, we can produce a motion that is fluid, coordinated, and dynamic. In turn, that will generate the maximum amount of clubhead speed in the downswing, as you hit through the ball to a high and stable finish.

A light grip is essential to building good movement.

Assuming the stance and feeling connected

Here you can see the arms, hands, and upper torso moving together, both on the back and forward swings.

Rear angle connection

A light connection of the upper arms and body aid a consistent movement.

But if you lose that feeling of connection at the beginning of the swing – I cannot stress this enough! – the entire action will fall apart and you will suffer a horrible experience when you hit the ball.

STAYING CONNECTED

The vast majority of golfers I see tend to move their arms and hands independently of the rest of their body, or upper torso. That is why they struggle for consistency in their swing.

Even those who have been taught or have read about the connected swing – and try to practice it – sometimes go to the opposite extreme. They interpret the idea of connection as meaning you must lock everything together, rather than just moving the various parts of the body together. Both variations ensure that a golfer will never reach his or her full potential.

ONLY HALFWAY

Connection will not work unless you are relaxed and can maintain a feeling of lightness throughout your upper body. And without good rhythm and tempo, you will have the lightness, but no dynamic movement.

Remember, the backswing merely sets up the full swing. Do it right, and you're halfway there. But only halfway. As Bobby Jones said, you don't hit the ball on the backswing.

LOW AND SLOW

The best advice I can give initially to promote the idea of the connected swing, while also establishing a nice sense of rhythm and tempo, is to start the takeaway – or what I like to call the first move – with the clubhead being taken back from the ball very low and slow. Start the club back low to the ground – about an inch or two above the turf – and move as slowly as comfortable, concentrating on a smooth movement. What this does is promote the idea of the arms, hands, shoulders, and upper torso moving back together and the club staying on the proper line. A movement that is slow and smooth, rather than quick or jerky, keeps all your body parts together, avoiding the tendency of many golfers to snatch the club away with their hands. At the same time, taking the club back low to the ground helps widen your swing arc, and thus allows the bigger muscles of your body to impart more power to the ball later in the throughswing.

TRIANGLE-CENTER DRILL

◆ ◆ ◆ ◆ ◆

I teach a certain drill to ingrain the idea of connection throughout the swing. Choke down on a club (i.e. grasp it further down the shaft than normal) and place the butt end against your body, somewhere between the navel and sternum – whatever feels most comfortable. Then practice moving the club away from an imaginary ball until the clubhead is about waist high.

IF YOU do this drill correctly, it will give you a strong impression of how the hands, arms, shoulders, and upper torso ought to move away together from the ball – and how they work together as a unit.

But the most important part of this drill to note is that the last thing to reach a finished position at waist-high is the clubhead! Did that surprise you?

If it did, then you are like most golfers. You have been swinging with the hands and arms, rather than the body. But in this exercise, it is the connection that moves the clubhead to its destination. Probably, in the past, you have been moving the clubhead in a way that leaves your body catching up rather than driving the action of the backswing.

It is now time to reverse that damaging tendency.

TAIL WAGS THE DOG

Jimmy Ballard, the famous golf guru, describes this initial move as a way of maintaining a feeling of the 'triangle and center.' He, and others such as the legendary Ben Hogan, have traditionally taught that, at address, the relationship between the shoulders, arms, and hands should form a triangle that remains unbroken throughout the entire swing.

This simple exercise will help you understand just how the arms, hands, and upper torso work together in the rotation back and through.

Triangle center drill

Triangle center drill – rear angle

With the butt of a club against your torso, you will sense how the body's 'center' – or the middle of the upper torso – stays in harmony with that triangle.

In other words, the large muscles of the upper torso move in conjunction with the arms, hands, and shoulders in the connected swing, pulling the clubhead back and through the ball.

Put yet another way by David Leadbetter, the 'tail wags the dog.'

THE ONE-PIECE TAKEAWAY

Perhaps you've heard the first move described differently – as the 'one-piece takeaway.' This is a term that I think confuses many golfers, because they inevitably interpret it by almost pushing the club back with the hands, arms, and shoulder joints. Do that, and the only way to raise the club fully is by cocking the wrists too soon, and in a way that lifts the arms across the chest.

Thus, you are making the first move without the center of your upper torso being involved, and you are breaking the connection I want you to strive to maintain. The first move in the golf swing must be made with the triangle of hands, arms, and shoulders in unison with the center of the upper body.

SUPPLE AND CONNECTED

When the club is waist-high in the backswing, the left arm should be comfortably extended and supple, so that if someone came along and pulled the club down to where you would normally grip it, you would remain connected and have a full extension of the clubhead.

At the same time, the right arm is starting to move away from the body and fold naturally.

If you were to continue the backswing here, the right arm would establish a triangle with the left up to the top of the swing, further mirroring our position at address when viewed from behind.

The triangle center drill also helps you to appreciate just where the club should be halfway back and halfway through in your swing. Perform this exercise regularly to develop the correct movement of your body.

If the arms work independently of the upper torso and rotation does not occur, the result will be a choppy swing resulting in a sliced, pulled, or skied golf shot.

PRACTICING THE CONNECTED SWING

◆ ◆ ◆ ◆ ◆

Now let's put triangle-center drill to good use in the swing.
Swing the club back to the waist-high position and stop.

I T MAY feel odd having the butt of a club against your chest, while also assuming the position of such a short swing. But, beyond that, any discomfort or restriction you might sense is really because you've probably never swung a golf club in the correct manner before!

In other words, you have never taken the club away from the ball in the first move of the backswing with your hands, arms, shoulders, and upper torso working together in the connected swing.

Now try doing the drill again without consciously keeping the butt of the club against your chest. Within a foot of moving away from the ball, I would bet the butt of the club has already parted company with your body. You are back to your usual swing. You are making the first move with the hands, arms, and shoulders, while your upper torso lags behind or doesn't move at all.

Instead of a connected swing, if your movement is a series of independent moving parts, your swing will lack consistency.

PRACTICE CORRECTLY

So go back to practicing the drill correctly, doing it over and over again to ingrain the idea of the connected swing. Use a long mirror if you have one, or better still, videotape yourself and note the progress you make.

I want you to concentrate on the idea of 'connectedness.' Think about how the body – in this case the upper torso – moves the hands, arms, and shoulders, rather than the other way around.

Note also how your weight shifts back to your right foot and your left knee turns back toward the right – which I'll discuss further later.

COCKING THE WRISTS

Perhaps you are wondering why I have not mentioned the role of the wrists in the first move of the backswing.

If you are an experienced player, I'm sure you've heard golfers talk endlessly about how and when to cock their wrists in the

This is a great exercise to develop good rotation on the correct plane. Take your posture first and then practice turning while at the same time staying bent over. It is important not to lift up or dip down, just rotate.

Practicing the connected swing

Connected swing close-ups

backswing. Or maybe they talk about how to manipulate their hands in the throughswing, especially at impact if they are trying to hit something other than their normal shot – say a draw.

You may have even been given some 'friendly' advice such as this during a round, delivered with the guarantee that it will improve your game immediately.

PASSIVE HANDS
Forget anything and everything you have ever heard about cocking the wrists and turning the hands!

The hands remain *passive* during a connected swing. They respond to everything else being done correctly. In a properly connected backswing, the right arm will begin to fold naturally as you reach

waist-high, and the momentum you are starting to build with the club will cause a natural hinging of the wrists.

If the club is gripped in the correct manner, and your swing is connected – with the triangle taken back with the center – the wrists are set in the proper position automatically.

Never make a conscious effort to cock or otherwise turn your wrists during the golf swing. Never!

The natural hinging of the wrists will occur if you maintain a light pressure in your grip. As you rotate, your right arm will fold naturally as shown above.

Below left: The momentum of the swing will cause your wrists to cock naturally.

Below: In a perfect takeaway there should be no hand action as you initiate your swing.

Perfect takeaway

POWER AND CONTROL IN THE CONNECTED SWING

◆ ◆ ◆ ◆ ◆

Shifting your weight correctly is a key to building a powerful swing. In order to understand this, you should resume the position you had with the club waist-high in the triangle-center drill (described in the previous pages) with its butt pressed against your chest.

THE CONNECTION you've established should have caused the left knee to break in well behind the spot where you would have set-up to the ball, and your weight should have shifted until it is predominantly on the inside of the right foot, or at least over the right foot from about the center to the heel.

If neither is the case, go back and do this again until you feel the proper weight shift and can establish that position – while also keeping the right knee as flexed as it was at address.

Now swing through to a waist-high finish – or put another way, swivel forward to face your intended target. You should feel your weight shift completely to your left foot – and that the weight has come off your right foot, which may have lifted off the ground, or could do so with little or no effort.

I hope that you will also now be starting to gain the sense that the throughswing *mirrors* the backswing.

CLUBHEAD POSITION

If you perform the triangle-center drill correctly – including a proper weight shift – you will also see that the clubhead is in the right position, both when you take the club back, and when you swing it through.

Assuming that you had the clubhead square at address, and did not manipulate your wrists, you should find that at waist level in the backswing, the toe of the club points upward to the sky, with the leading edge perpendicular to the ground. The

clubhead should be in the same position at waist-high in the throughswing. In other words, the clubhead is square.

OPEN TOE

However, if you find that at waist-level in the backswing, the toe is open – or pointing behind you and facing up – you did not maintain your connection in the swing and you probably tried to dictate what your wrists were doing.

By the same token, if you find that the face of the clubhead is pointing toward the

Weight transfer

ground, or closed, in the throughswing, you have also broken your connection between the triangle and center.

The important thing to realize here is that doing this will make any chance of returning the clubhead square to the ball at impact considerably more difficult. Plus, you will lack the proper coil behind the ball, because you have shortened the arc of your swing.

That almost inevitably leads to various mishaps – as you instinctively struggle to square the club with your hands. It will also certainly produce a lack of power in the swing.

BODY LEVERAGE

The point of all this is to introduce you to the idea of body leverage in the connected swing. By using your body to swing the golf club, you create power and consistency. This will give you a much stronger movement through the ball and you will not have to exert as much energy.

Watch the average golfer at the range. Within minutes, he's grunting and sweating. Does your favorite pro do that? When he or she swings, the effort looks minimal, and yet the result is a powerful, controlled shot –

essentially, what we mean by the phrase 'playing within yourself.'

LOSS OF CONTROL

But most golfers, whether consciously or not, think they can create power through their arms and wrists. They try to whack the daylights out of the ball, short-circuiting any input of the larger muscles of the body. This has several negative consequences, the most common one being a disconnection of the swing, and thus a loss of control over the clubhead.

If your swing is dominated by the hands and arms, the clubface will open and close too quickly and you will not be able to visualize where it is at any particular point of the swing. The tendency to try and compensate for a clubhead in the wrong position is extremely difficult to resist, and a lack of consistency will dominate your ball-striking.

When you use a connected swing, you are moving the clubhead in tune with your body, and it will open and close much more slowly and be in the proper place throughout the swing. In effect, there is less to do, and less to worry about, in the connected swing – and the result will be greater consistency.

The rotation of your body combined with the transfer of your weight from right foot to left foot is the engine of your golf swing. If you want a powerful, elegant, and efficient golf swing, learn and practice good body rotation and weight transfer. Observe players like Tiger Woods – he is without doubt the best golfer in the world because he understands body leverage and connection.

HEAD ROTATION IN THE CONNECTED SWING

◆ ◆ ◆ ◆ ◆

The first move away from the ball will break down if the golfer becomes fixated on the ball by trying to keep his or her head still or down. Your goal should be simply to allow your head to rotate freely with your body rotation.

DON'T ALLOW the ball to become the absolute target. Think about your swing, and where you want the ball to go, rather than the ball itself – partly by not staring fixedly at the ball, and partly by letting your head rotate slightly on the backswing.

SIMPLY TERRIFIED

But we often forget this. Standing over that little white orb, we are sometimes reluctant – or plain terrified in the case of most beginners – to turn the body, and thus the head as well, behind it.

We are afraid of losing visual contact. It's so tempting to remain with both eyes fixed on the ball, staring down in the hope that doing so will ensure we can bring the clubface back into contact with the ball and therefore hit a reasonable shot.

But the opposite will be the result, because failing to move the head at all will prevent the correct body movement – and destroy any hope of a connected swing. So forget everything you've ever heard about keeping your head still!

HEAD ROTATION

Not moving the head is one of the great myths in golf. In fact, the head must rotate slightly back, or to the right, along with the upper torso in the connected swing.

So, that feeling of lightness should extend to our neck muscles as well. They should be relaxed. They should be receptive to movement. Keeping the head in a fixed position, or square to the ball, will cause the swing to break down as the left arm folds up and collapses, reducing any chance of imparting real power to the ball. That's

In order for your body to rotate back and through, allow your head to move with your body. At the top of the backswing you should only be able to see the ball through your left eye, the head should then rotate through so that you finish looking at the target.

Correct head movement

Address.

Top of backswing.

Just after impact.

Finish position.

Head-down disaster

Forcing your head to remain still or down on a golf shot is the worst thing you can do.

because you will be unable to turn fully behind the ball and so you will reduce the width of your swing arc.

HEAD MYTHS

I wonder where the myth of the 'steady' head came from, or what other commentators sometimes refer to as keeping the 'head down.'

The correct practice has always been not to keep the head still, but to keep some visual contact with the ball – acting on the basis of that other old adage 'keep your eye on the ball!'

This maxim really does apply, although what we actually want to happen is to see the ball with only – and I emphasize 'only' – the corner of our left eye. You can test this by taking a practice swing and closing your left eye at the top of your backswing. If you can still see the ball, you've got a major swing fault, and there is certainly no 'connection' in your swing.

Again, you have not turned fully and your swing arc is narrow.

SWING TRIGGER

All the great players move their head in the backswing, some more than others – but certainly all of them! Jack Nicklaus often tells the story of his first teacher holding his hair to keep him from turning his head. But in fact, Jack does turn his head, though in his case, he moves it before he starts the backswing, pre-setting it so the corner of his left eye is over the ball before he starts his movement. For Nicklaus, that move is a swing 'trigger.'

LATERAL MOVEMENT

These days, several great players not only rotate their heads to keep their swings connected, but they also work on a slight lateral movement of the head. Tiger Woods is a good example. By the time he has set his powerful swing at the top, his nose is just over the inside of his back foot, with his head very much behind the golf ball.

So before you even start the swing, tell yourself that your head will move. Allow for the natural rotation of the head as the upper torso moves to the right and back, allowing the body to coil behind the ball. Then forget everything you have ever been told about trying to keep your head still.

Lateral movement makes good striking impossible.

NEW TOOLS OF THE TRADE

Having a friend videotape your swing is really the only way to check your head position during the entire movement. New computer software I now use in teaching my own pupils even allows for multiple images of your swing, including those shot from various angles, to be studied on the screen simultaneously.

This marvellous tool also offers the option of comparing what you are doing with images of other golfers. I like to take shots of various golf pros practicing on the range, then compare these images with those of my pupils, focusing on players who have a similar build and physique.

THE FOUNDATION OF YOUR SWING

◆ ◆ ◆ ◆ ◆

Another point that often gets overlooked before we even start our swing is the role of the lower body. As I described in the previous section on set-up and stance, your weight should be distributed from the balls of your feet to your heels, and it should remain this way to provide a solid, balanced foundation for the entire swing.

B UT MANY golfers get utterly fixated on their hands and the ball sitting below them on the tee or grass. And since they are holding the golf club in their hands – and the clubhead is poised near the ball – that's where most of their attention is directed.

They are concentrating only on what they can see right in front of them!

SUPPLE LEGS

I try to have a definite sense of my legs supporting me from below – supple, and yet firmly in contact with Mother Earth, and, of course, connected to the rest of my body.

If you do not have this feeling of support, your central nervous system is liable to interpret that as a sign of instability down below. And if that message is sent to the brain, the result will be a certain rigidity, as your body rejects any idea of cutting loose in a strong, athletic movement.

I liken this to standing on one leg. If you do that, your body will try to find a way to brace itself to overcome the feeling of instability, and this will certainly prevent you from doing anything as powerful and dynamic as swinging a golf club, for fear of the obvious result – you will lose your balance and topple over!

Your legs play a crucial role in anchoring your swing. Like a building, a golf swing needs a stable foundation.

Lower body

Legs and support

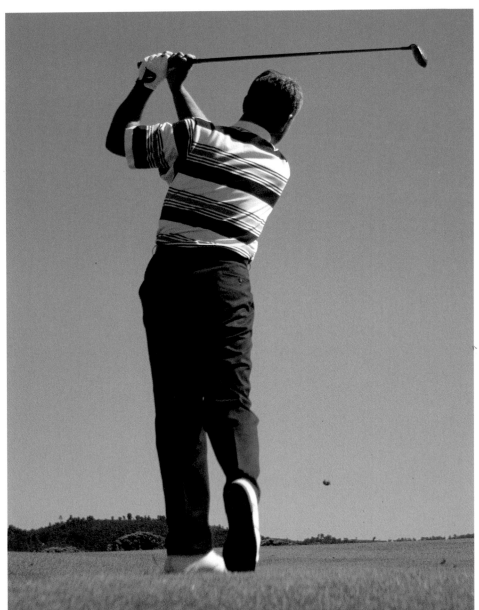

In order to maintain the plane of your golf swing and to brace the upper body rotation, your legs must retain the same flexed position as at address throughout the swing.

Below: If the lower body does not provide good support, loss of balance will be inevitable.

PUTTING IT ALL TOGETHER

◆◆◆◆◆

The correct backswing should feel more or less natural. The movement should be programmed into your mind and body. Let's go through the process together.

ONCE I know what my target is, I want to feel strong, relaxed, and prepared to make all the right moves. Then I initiate my first motion in the backswing by trying to keep things very smooth, with a continuous, easy flow of the hands, arms, shoulders, and upper torso away from the ball.

SIMPLE PICTURES

Picture the 'center-triangle' image again, with your shoulders forming the base, your arms the sides, and your hands the apex of the triangle. You want to keep this triangle intact as you start the backswing, relative to the center of your chest.

I trust that you've practiced the essential parts of the first move for hours, days, and perhaps even weeks or months! So, finally, it's time to simplify things. Just think in terms of maintaining the same basic position you had at address throughout the initial part of the first move.

In other words, you can now drop the idea of the 'center-triangle' specifically, and merely picture a mirror image of a good address position being held throughout the backswing.

DYNAMIC RESISTANCE

Meanwhile, the lower body will be braced and supporting your movement, with the weight starting to move onto your right foot and the hips gradually being pulled around by the turn of the upper torso.

Please note that I said the hips are turned around by the upper torso. They follow, rather than move simultaneously, or lead the action. If this movement is done correctly, a slight tension will begin to build between the hips and upper body – and, in this case, the tension is good, rather than bad.

Such tension is dynamic, the resistance that actually balances the whole backswing, while later providing – by opposition – a powerful coil as the body moves fully behind the ball and begins to build up the power you will later unleash through the golf ball.

COILED SPRING

What do I mean by coil? Think of your upper body as a spring, turning against the resistance of your hips and legs. At the top of the backswing, that spring should be fully wound up, ready to be unleashed – or sprung – in a powerful throughswing that fires through the ball to a high and balanced finish.

But as you proceed through your backswing, keep in mind that your hips actually end their rotation at roughly one-half the turn of the shoulders and upper torso.

Remember also that it is the upper torso that pulls the hips around. They do not rotate at the same time or pace as the upper body. In fact, they are the last major part of the body to move in the initial phase of the backswing.

WEIGHT TRANSFER

Weight transfer is also a vital part of the backswing. I want to transfer most of my weight to the right foot as I rotate or turn back from the ball. By the time I finish the first move, about 90 per cent of my weight should be over the back foot, distributed from the center to the heel.

At the same time, my right knee should remain braced and flexed, just as it was in my set-up. This provides the support I need to hold my position at the top, although that will only take a matter of a few split seconds in real time.

Meanwhile, my left foot has stayed on the ground, although for many golfers that isn't the case! A little lift of the foot here is acceptable, as long as you do not become unbalanced. Ben Hogan said that he did not care if a golfer raised his left foot in the backswing or not. And some of the great players had a pronounced lift in their front foot. But, if at all possible, keep your left foot planted. As you will see in the next section, it is one of the keys to a powerful, athletic swing.

To become a good golfer you need to study the previous pages so that your backswing can be produced automatically. Then, when faced with that pressure shot, you will instinctively believe in your movement.

SPINE ANGLE AND SWING PLANE

◆ ◆ ◆ ◆ ◆

When you take your position at address, you have effectively preset your spine in a certain alignment – what pros call the 'spinal angle.' As you rotate your body in the swing, it is absolutely essential that the angle you have created at address is maintained throughout the swing – so there is absolutely no lifting or lowering of the spine.

I F THE spine angle varies, it will have a very detrimental effect on your ability to bring the club back through the ball toward the target. So it's essential to maintain the spinal angle that you created at address.

FIXED AXIS

Picture an imaginary line drawn down your back, from the top of your head to your hips. As you begin your backswing, you are rotating your spine around that angle, or line, turning back and then forward, simply opening and closing your body in relation to this fixed axis.

It is similar to a door hanging on an angle from a pair of hinges – opening and closing. That is how the body turns along the spinal angle, both in the backswing, and as we unwind through the ball.

At the same time, your shoulder turn should remain perpendicular to your spine, and your shoulders turn on a level plane, with the hips on roughly the same line. This is what we call the 'swing plane,' and it both follows from, and is connected to, the spinal angle.

IN THE SLOT

What do I mean by 'swing plane?' Ben Hogan was one of the most consistent strikers of the ball in the history of the game. But even he struggled to 'slot' his club into the proper position at the top of the

Above: Developing a consistent swing plane is very much part of becoming a consistent striker of the ball.

Left: Your posture will determine your eventual swing plane, therefore make sure you're in a good position before taking the club back.

A simple way to understand the swing plane is to swing the club at a target, in this case my hand, positioned at different levels, starting at head height and working down to the ball.

backswing until he understood the idea of 'plane.'

Once he grasped that concept and practiced swinging the club along this imaginary line, he gained enough confidence to rely on his swing in the pressure of competition and eventually to become a winner of golf's most coveted trophies.

Imagine a pane of glass extending from the ball to your shoulders, with your head poking through a hole at the top. The angle of this plane will vary depending on your height and the distance that you stand from the ball, producing what we often refer to as either a steep or shallow plane.

STAYING ON PLANE

But one thing is constant. There is no such thing as a swing that is too steep or too shallow if the golfer consistently swings his shoulders along the line of the plane. Like the spinal angle, any variation above or below the plane will put the swing out of position and produce a bad shot. But staying on the same plane throughout the swing will groove an excellent movement.

Try to think about both your spinal angle and swing plane when practicing your backswing. Getting both right is one of the essential ingredients to making that first move correctly.

Once you're confident you can make that first move, you'll be like a sprinter who is poised and ready to explode out of the blocks when the gun goes.

REFLECTIONS ON SWING PLANE

You can check to see if your swing plane is correct simply by looking in a mirror. Pick a spot on the floor where your ball would normally be in your address position, then swing a 5- or 6-iron back, holding it at the top. If an imaginary line drawn from the butt end of your grip to the ball falls across your left shoulder, your swing plane is too upright. This means you probably return the clubface to the ball in an open position, take deep divots, and often sky the ball. If the imaginary line cuts across your navel, your swing plane is too flat and you probably return the clubface in a closed position, resulting in many shots hit too low and hot.

The correct – or neutral – swing plane places the imaginary line directly across the right shoulder. From there, you will return the clubface square at impact and strike the ball more consistently.

THE THROUGHSWING

◆◆◆◆◆

With the body coiled and ready to unleash the clubhead at high speed, the release of power into the ball on the throughswing can either be an exhilarating experience or an embarrassing hack.

THE THROUGHSWING

◆ ◆ ◆ ◆ ◆

Now it is crunch time. The transition from the top of the backswing to the start of the throughswing is the most crucial split second in golf – and the ultimate moment of truth.

EITHER THE golfer will take advantage of having achieved an excellent position at the top of the backswing – with the body fully rotated and powerfully coiled behind the ball – or the golfer will now destroy all his or her previous good work.

Done properly, the throughswing will unleash the clubhead at high speed – the pros hit the ball at over 100mph (161km/h) – smacking into surlyn or balata to send the object of our desire flying high and true toward the target.

TAKING SHORTCUTS

On the other hand – and I choose that phrase deliberately – the golfer may make a terrible hack of the job, not only embarrassing himself, but perhaps doing permanent damage to his score. How many times have you seen a fellow golfer make a nice backswing, only to snatch the club back at the ball or fail to hit through it?

Unfortunately, human nature is such that the failure of most amateur golfers is caused by rushing – they are trying to shortcut the downswing. They're nervous. They want to get to the ball as soon as they can. So almost instinctively, they fall back on old habits, bringing the club down with their hands and arms, rather than using their body.

LOOKING EASY

The transition phase from the backswing to hitting through the ball must be a dynamic, athletic move, fully utilizing the body in a coordinated fashion that is seemingly unhurried, and outwardly graceful.

Think of Ronaldo scoring a goal. Pete Sampras hitting an ace. Michael Jordan sinking the winning basket. There's no wasted motion, and no excessive exertion. In

A simple baseball type action is good practice when you are first developing the correct turning motion though the ball.

Practicing the baseball swing

The throughswing – bad followthrough

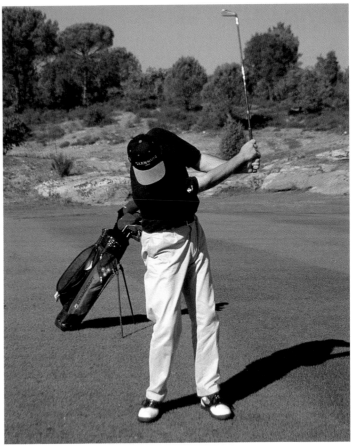

other words, they make it look easy – even if it surely is anything but easy.

UNCOILING THE SWING

So, learning how to perform the throughswing is a case of disciplining the body and brain through practice. The golfer must know what is about to happen, and how he or she should proceed.

Simply put, the throughswing is a reverse image of the backswing, as the legs, hips, upper torso, shoulders, arms, and hands gradually uncoil piece by piece. At the same time, there is a slight lateral weight shift to the left, as the majority of the weight moves from the back foot to the front.

In other words, the swing uncoils in exactly the same order as it was previously coiled up, so that the last thing to go back, is the first thing to come forward.

IMAGE AND FEEL

Think about that for a moment. Images and a physical feeling for what we do in golf are vitally important. Once again, I would suggest that you initially practice this motion in front of a mirror with a club, but no ball. That's the best way to help you prepare for what you'll do later on the practice range – and ultimately the course.

I like to focus on the impression of the backswing uncoiling like a tightly wound

spring into the full swing. I firmly believe that if you can think of this move in that way, it will help to unravel any mystery attached to the throughswing – and help it unfold in a logical sequence.

Don't stay down with the ball too long, otherwise you'll get trapped behind the ball.

PAUSE AT THE TOP

One of the most common faults of the average golfer is the tendency to hit from the top – or initiate the throughswing with the shoulders, rather than allowing them to uncoil gradually after the lower body starts to move back to the left. The legendary Tommy Armour, a Scot who emigrated to America in the 20s and won 24 golf tournaments in two decades – including both the US and British Open – developed the most famous cure for hitting from the top – a split-second pause at the top of the backswing. In his 1953 book *How to Play Your Best Golf All the Time*, he wrote that adding this pause was the 'greatest single aid' to eliminating what he saw as the 'worst fault in the golf swing.'

Next time you are at the golf range, try Armour's technique and see if it doesn't help improve the timing of your throughswing.

THE FIRST MOVE FORWARD

◆ ◆ ◆ ◆ ◆

It can be difficult to keep the first move in the throughswing under control
— just as it was difficult to make that first move in the backswing. When
most golfers realize that they have arrived at, or near, the top of their
backswing, they suddenly want to get the clubhead to the ball as
quickly as possible.

S O RELAX, there's no need to rush, the ball isn't going away. The throughswing has to be smooth, so that the body can uncoil fluidly and pull the clubhead through, rather than the other way around.

FIRST MOVE FORWARD

Remember that as you coiled your body up in the backswing, your upper torso and shoulders rotated back, your weight shifted from your left to your right side, and your legs provided balance and support for the entire movement. At the same time, this coiling motion pulled in the left knee, inclining it toward the back leg, while the hips were gradually pulled around to half the rotation of the shoulder turn.

Therefore, the first part of the body that should come forward to start the throughswing is that left side. I believe that a slight lateral movement of the left hip toward the target is the ideal trigger for your throughswing. In the past, men no less eminent than Ben Hogan and Bobby Jones also thought that the forward turning of the hips was the trigger, or first move, that initiated the throughswing.

Other golf pros and swing gurus maintain it is actually a separation of the left knee from the right, the shift of weight onto the left foot.

It is difficult to focus precisely on individual actions, since they happen so quickly and everyone has their own way of sensing this motion. On top of this, any

A slight lateral movement with the left hip toward the target initiates the forward move. As your hips rotate to face the target, your upper body and clubhead will be pulled forward developing tremendous centrifugal force.

The forward move

The lower body

Left: The forward drive of your lower body is an essential part of developing a powerful golf swing.

Below: In order to develop the correct motion through impact, practice turning your left hip to the left whilst at the same time swinging the right hand toward the target.

swing that is truly athletic will be partly instinctive, and therefore vary slightly from golfer to golfer. The way a golfer perceives the sequence of what happens will inevitably vary.

UNCOILING THE BODY

Suffice it to say that both the hips and the left knee move more or less simultaneously in the first split second of the throughswing and weight is transferred to the front foot. The essential point remains that the body must uncoil gradually, roughly from the ground up, in reverse order to the backswing coil – with the movement of the clubhead always coming last.

If you watch a slow-motion videotape of a good swing, you will see that indeed there is a pronounced separation of the left knee from the right in the initial part of the throughswing. Roughly at the same time, the hips and upper torso are beginning to uncoil as well, pulling through the shoulders and arms as the weight transfers smoothly from the right foot to the left.

The overall effect is that these actions allow the body to rotate around the left heel into the final part of the swing.

FORWARD POWER AND DRIVE

The way I like to think of this first move, and the way I teach it to my golfing pupils, is by telling them they are trying to develop a strong sense of forward power and drive, thus imparting that energy to the ball. This starts with a slight lateral movement of the left hip, which goes forward toward the target, then this translates into a rotational movement that pulls the body around, letting it eventually open up fully to face the chosen target.

But let me emphasize one thing in particular. This action must be done in the most non-violent way possible! The initiation of the throughswing should be an easy and fluid move, because if you turn the left hip – or anything else for that matter – too aggressively, the club will be thrown outside the correct line and you'll hack at the ball with an out-to-in swingpath, probably slicing it as a result.

Remember, the uncoiling of the body into the throughswing should be a natural movement that you do not force, hurry, or try to push. A good way of thinking about this is to focus on the idea of simply *letting it happen*.

THE THROUGHSWING FROM IMPACT TO FINISH

♦ ♦ ♦ ♦ ♦

An essential ingredient of both the backswing and throughswing movement is the efficient transfer of weight. To initiate the throughswing, the golfer has to get his or her weight back over to the left side in order to unleash the swing and provide power to the clubhead.

USING A slight lateral slide as the hips begin to turn and the knees separate, you rotate over the left heel, holding the club lightly and simply letting it swing through. In effect, you allow the club to pull you. And if that happens, you're really in business. But if you start pushing the club in any way, you'll have serious problems.

HARD WORK

What do I mean by pushing the club? Instead of allowing the club to swing freely with light hands and wrists, many golfers try to muscle the clubhead into the ball, which inevitably means that they are holding the club too tightly and forcing all the action. In other words, instead of the club doing what it was designed to do – how many times have you heard this one – you do all the work!

Of course, your reward for all that hard work is a golfing disaster.

CLUB PULL

Try to hold the club as lightly as possible and allow the left hip to ease its way around in the throughswing. Don't try to be aggressive. Let your weight naturally move onto the left heel, and set the clubhead free.

If you have done this correctly, and allowed the club to swing freely, centrifugal force will come into play and pull the arms to full extension.

Yes, the club will actually pull you, and you might even be able to feel the right shoulder being brought through under your chin to its finish point.

IMPACT!

What happens when the clubhead finally smacks into the ball?

The answer may surprise you – very little that you need worry about! In fact, if you've done everything correctly up to this point, the clubhead will merely zip through the ball and send it 300 yards or more – if you're Tiger Woods, that is.

In addition, any conscious effort to manipulate the hands or wrists will only lead to trouble. At the impact position, you can do precious little to control the clubhead, because everything is happening too fast. Rely instead on a sound grip, your preparation, and the proper execution of your swing to allow the clubhead to do the work at this stage of the game.

PRACTICE IMAGES

I would suggest focusing on several images that you might conjure up when practicing. These will help you to visualize your position at impact, and how you groove your movement through the ball.

First, you want to think of swinging through the ball as something like throwing underhand to a target, roughly like skimming a stone across a pond. The right arm is at first coiled backward and raised, then swings forward with the wrist providing that extra momentum as the stone or ball is released.

Here you can see the throughswing in action. The hips are turning left and the club is released toward the target.

At the same time, the elbow passes close to the right hip and finishes with full extension or beyond.

Practice doing this with a tennis ball, a stone or whatever is available to give you the right feeling, then grab a club and swing it to waist-high. Think about the right hand turning over the left on the throughswing – once past impact.

As the body continues to rotate to the left, the club is literally pulling the golfer through to a complete follow-through.

TWO-HANDED PASS

Of course, you really want to swing as freely as possible with both hands through impact. One way of ingraining this idea is to practice with a medicine ball if you can obtain one, or at least a football, basketball, or even a beach ball. The idea is to imagine you are making a two-handed pass with the ball, from the right side of the body to the left, with the object being to get the ball to a target. Doing this will resemble the motion of the golf swing.

Hold the ball in front of you and take your address position. Then begin a simulated backswing. You will automatically shift your weight from the left foot to the right, which builds up your power, then reverse the action as you fling the ball toward the target.

NATURAL POWER

This exercise will give you the idea of how you can naturally generate power in the swing through simple body leverage, with the hands and arms serving as conduits of that energy. In the end, your body rotation will carry you all the way around to the left, in exactly the same way as the club does in a good swing.

But remember that at impact, your technique is what you must ultimately rely upon. If you make a good backswing, and unleash your throughswing in the proper sequence, you will generate energy and power at the point of contact, with the centrifugal force I mentioned in the previous section controlling much of what happens through the ball.

THE FINISHED POSITION

How do we get to the finish of the throughswing? Simply put, the rotation of your torso and shoulders continues until your hips are fully turned and your chest faces the target, the body having fully rotated around your left heel.

That's the part that should be common to everyone. And yet every golfer has his own version of the finish, and they can vary dramatically. Some are unusual, and some are absolute works of art. Think of Arnold Palmer. Then think of Ernie Els.

The point here is that while no two golfers finish their swing in quite the same

Swinging a heavy object such as a medicine ball, or in this case a cool-box, helps develop the feeling of the arms and body working together throughout the movement.

Although the throughswing is very much about freedom and letting the club 'go,' the relationship of the arms and body remains constant.

way, they all tell us something about what went on before. They provide an insight both into a golfer's strengths and weaknesses. And they give us clues as to how we might enhance the good points, while fixing the faults, in our own swings.

MAINTAIN THE FINISH

I always tell the golfers that I teach to maintain their finished position for a few seconds. You want to do so because:

• If you anticipate finishing up with a balanced, controlled follow-through, that will have a positive effect right through your golf swing.
• Your swing faults will become apparent. If you fall forward at the finish, for instance, you will discover that you did not shift your weight properly and you were not balanced.

COUNT TO THREE

Again, it is a matter of programming the body and brain to know what they are trying to achieve together. Such visualization techniques work on the subconscious. Thinking about balance and control will impart the proper idea while you are actually moving the club.

In addition, I suggest that at the end of the golf swing, you should hold the finish and count, 1-2-3. But rather than thinking of this as a finale, remember that the real action in golf is only just beginning. As you count, the imaginary ball has started to rise into the air and fly toward your target.

EXHILARATING SWINGS

If you have done everything I have described in this section and the previous one properly, the experience of hitting a golf ball *will* ultimately be exhilarating, rather than embarrassing. In short, you will have released the power in your swing, and found the key to unlocking your potential for the game of golf.

But before we conclude our examination of the swing – and you try to take my techniques to the course – please read the following pages. There, I pull together everything I have explained about the backswing and throughswing, then round it off with a few more mental images. I also offer some final tips and thoughts on the central action of the game – your golf swing.

As the swing continues through, the pictures above featuring both cool-box and golf club show how the arms, hands, and torso maintain the relationship that began at address.

REPLACE THE BALL

◆◆◆◆◆

As I've already explained, Nick Faldo spent the first two months of his golfing life developing his golf swing without a golf ball. When he began hitting balls, he had already created a swing that consistently propelled the clubhead toward the target.

WHAT IS the natural extension of the concept of removing the ball? My own golf instructor, Ian Connelly, used to repeat one basic rule over and over again to me. Only after you have learned how to swing the club properly are you ready to bring the ball back into play – and, finally, into its proper role.

In other words, you have now ingrained the idea into your mind and body that the swing is the central action of golf, and that it should be your principal focus – not the act of hitting at the ball. So after you've developed a dynamic, athletic swing – just put the ball in the way.

Let me repeat that: just put the ball in the way.

A good golf swing is one in which the ball is simply in the path of the clubhead. The ball is not your target – you merely swing through it, with no conscious effort to hit it. If you can master that concept, you have taken one of the biggest steps possible toward finding your own complete swing.

INSTINCTIVE GOLF

Like the little child who grabs the club and swings away with youthful abandon, you have to learn (or re-learn) how to be instinctive about your swing. An excellent swing links physical know-how and mental application, then tosses away the conscious mindset of the technician.

What do I mean by that? By now, your swing should be mechanically sound, but also programmed in your subconscious, with the whole process written into your muscle

A much improved swing

Exercise

REMOVE THE BALL

Former Ryder Cup captain Bernard Gallacher recommends that golfers always turn the brand name on the ball down to avoid fixing visually on the ball, especially when teeing up. This way, the golfer sees only a clean, white area. Any number of problems can result when a player stares at the ball. He or she might limit their lateral movement in both the backswing and throughswing, or the head may come down, creating a rocking or tilting action. Gallacher says he tries to play with a simple awareness that the ball is below him, almost seeing the ball only in his subconscious.

Left: Repetition is the mother of skill. And remember quality is better than quantity so practice good swings again and again.

Above left: If you can't practice regularly, perform simple loosening exercises that remind your body of the correct movement.

memory and throughout your body. Of course, unless you continue to practice, any consistency that you have achieved up to this point will start to deteriorate.

REPETITION AND SKILL

Go back to what I said before. You must swing the club in slow motion, over and over and over again, without the golf ball. Far too many golfers fall into the trap of thinking they have learned something, and then immediately head out to the range, eager to whack a couple of dozen golf balls.

Avoid that trap like the plague. If you try to short-circuit the process, it will be disastrous for the development of your swing. You have to develop a pattern, and that takes hundreds of hours. Repetition is the mother of skill.

That is how to become both consistent, and to learn how to *not* think about the ball and the parts of the swing. In other words, how to make the swing instinctive again.

HOW TO PRACTICE

◆◆◆◆◆

Most golfers cannot wait to start letting fly with a bucket of golf balls after they have read one magazine article on swing technique, taken a few lessons, or tried a new grip. That's a surefire recipe for failure.

EVEN IF you do hit a few good shots, it would be a mistake to believe you have mastered a new swing, or some aspect of a new swing. More than likely, you'll probably hit a lot of indifferent shots after the initial excitement wears off. And again, it would be a mistake to think that fact means anything, either good or bad.

You have to practice each new aspect of the swing for a considerable period of time before you can incorporate it into a practice routine, and certainly long before you can take it to the course.

DRIVING RANGE TIPS

Do go to the driving range, although, once there, try not to hit too many golf balls! Take lots of practice swings instead. And use an easy club like a 6-iron, rather than the driver, for an extended time. After you have built up some confidence, and an understanding of what you are trying to accomplish, then you can pull out other clubs, trying to groove the same swing aspect with each.

Always aim at something when hitting balls on the driving range, and vary the targets. When you play, you are constantly confronted with a variety of situations, so why turn practice into a mere bash of the ball into the unknown?

Develop and practice a pre-shot routine at the range. All the top pros have a consistent routine that helps them visualize the shot, take aim, and relax before hitting the ball. Doing the same is a key to playing better. In addition, developing consistency in one area will work into other parts of your game.

TIME FOR SUCCESS

Pick a target, decide on what club to use and how to shape the shot, then visualize the ball moving along your target line and landing where you want it to go.

Move behind the ball to find an aiming point, using something a few inches ahead on the mat or grass.

Take your stance and give the club a waggle to loosen up before starting your backswing.

Finally, step back and see how many other people at the range are doing the same thing. Not many, I'll bet – out of shyness, impatience, or whatever – which is their mistake, not yours.

Now you're ready to take a shot. Go ahead, and succeed.

PRO TIP

Several famous golf gurus have suggested a shoulder turn of about 90 degrees to the target, with the hips turned half that amount. I agree with that basic ratio, as long as we keep the numbers approximate. Some players can turn only 75 degrees, and others 110 – it depends on individual flexibility. Big hitters such as John Daly turn more than 90 degrees. But even the pros turn less as they get older. Roughly speaking, the hips will turn half the amount that the upper torso does.

Left: The only person you never see in golf is yourself! That's why you need a good teacher.

Below: Practice with all your clubs hitting a variety of shots. This keeps it interesting, helps you to become more creative and encourages you to play and learn a variety of shots.

How to practice

Good = straight shot.

In-to-out = slice or push.

Out-to-in = hook or push

Above: Learn from your divot pattern – with clubs lined up on the ground it's easy to see if your swingpath at impact is good or bad.

CHIPPING AND PITCHING

◆◆◆◆◆

Devote 50 per cent of your practice time to these shots and your scores will improve dramatically.

CHIPPING AND PITCHING
◆◆◆◆◆

Have you ever played a round with a golf pro? If you have, you know what separates his or her game from yours. No, it's not that the professional golfer is generally two clubs better than you, that they can hit a driver nearly 300 yards, or even that their putting stroke is just that much more silky.

YOU KNOW the real difference. What makes the pro a better player is their short game. Put another way, it's how they correct errant shots. How they get the ball up and down for par after making that occasional, but inevitable, mistake. Meanwhile, when you go into a bunker, miss the green by a few feet, or face an awkward 40-yard (37m) pitch, you know you're probably heading for bogey (one over par) – at best.

The same holds true for the pros out on the various tours around the world. Think of today's leading stars, and who do you come up with? Men – and these days increasingly women – who combine awesome power off the tee with an exquisite short game. Pros like Tiger Woods, Ernie Els, David Duval, Colin Montgomerie, Laura Davies, Annika Sorenstam, and Karrie Webb.

They're all considered 'long,' but also have 'touch' around the greens.

THE REAL SECRET

Now you know the real secret of golf. In this section, and the following two (Bunker Play and Putting), I will show you how to play better from close in, a skill which can dramatically lower your scores.

But there's a catch. You'll have to practice these shots more than you probably do now, because here is where feel, and to some extent, imagination come into play. That does not come easily, though I guarantee that any extra time you spend perfecting these shots will more than pay off in the long run.

As Gary Player – one of the great short-game artists of all time – often says: 'The more I practice, the more I get lucky.'

THE STANDARD PITCH SHOT

This is a crucial shot for the average golfer for all the reasons stated above, but for one more in particular. Most high- to medium-

Below left: Pros often carry different types of wedges from the rest of their irons (3–9 irons). These wedges are often made of softer metal to help control the golf ball from short range.

Below: There are even different shafts made specially for wedges that are stiff flex and that maximize the feel of the clubhead.

range handicap players will generally miss at least 50-60 per cent of greens in regulation, and might have problems hitting the green in two on long par fours and certainly most par fives.

In each situation, the golfer is often faced with a third shot that a pro never has to play, which quite literally accounts for the 18 or so extra strokes that the average club player is given in the form of a handicap before his or her first tee shot on the first hole.

But here is where you can cut that margin down and start threatening the club championship, or at least move up in your local rankings. With a solid pitching stroke, you can start turning bogeys into pars, and pars into birdies.

FLOATING PITCH

How many times have you found yourself with 200 or more yards (185+m) to an elevated green for your second shot on those

Right: Ball position will vary depending on the height that you require on the pitch shot.

Right: The chip and run shot can be used if no hazards lie between you and your target.

Below: Practice will help you determine the length of swing required for various distances.

long par fours? And how many times have you faced an 85-100 yard (78–91m) shot on a par five for your third?

In the first case, most golfers would be advised to forget trying to hit the green in two and put that problematic fairway wood back in the bag, opting instead to hit a comfortable 7- or 8-iron to a spot around 100 yards (91m) or less into the green. Alternatively, with the modern development of utility woods, other players may opt to try a 7- or 9-wood and try to land within 40-60 yards (37–55m).

In both cases, you are now ready to float a high pitch shot onto the short grass. With practice, you should be able to land that pitch close enough to the pin to have a chance at making the putt.

PREPARATION FOR THE PITCH SHOT

◆◆◆◆◆

The pitch shot is really just a miniature version of a full swing. The ball is hit high because of the loft of the clubhead – usually traveling between about 35 and 100 yards (32 to 91m) – and goes farther in the air than it does along the ground.

THE MOST commonly used clubs to play the shot – depending on the distance to carry – are a sand wedge, pitching wedge, or 9-iron. In recent years, many golfers have also added a lob wedge to their bag, which is ideal for shorter pitches off a good lie.

SHORT BUT SWEET

Now for the tricky part, and the reason why you must spend more time practicing this shot than most others. The pitch is hit with an abbreviated version of the full swing, but the ball must still be hit firmly.

Put another way, although you are not swinging the club as far back as you would for a normal shot, you must still accelerate at the bottom of the swing, just as you would for a normal hit!

Without an authoritative swing, you will pull your punch, and the result will be a disastrous hit, a shot skulled over the green or one that trips along the grass seeking out a hazard. Now, instead of that par or birdie you envisioned, you're looking at bogey, double bogey, or even worse.

As a result, many golfers fear the pitch shot as much as any other in the game. But there's no reason for that fear if you understand how to execute the pitch.

THE STANDARD SET-UP

The key to making a good pitch shot is first to set-up well to the ball. Here, the stance is

Set up with your ball in the center of your stance and your hips and feet pointing slightly left of the target (open stance); your shoulders should remain parallel to the ball-to-target line. Your hands should be ahead of the golf ball and you can choke down on the club (by how much depends on the length of the shot).

Pitch shot technique

also a miniaturized version of what we use for a longer iron or wood, with some important differences.

The first difference is that the stance is 'open,' which means you pull your lead foot back from parallel to the target line by a few inches. At the same time, the back foot, hips, chest, and shoulders remain square, or parallel to the ball-to-target line.

The second difference is that the stance is narrower, with the outside of the feet at about shoulder-width for the average pitch. You'll remember that for a 5-iron, an imaginary line would run from the outside of your shoulders down to the inside of your heels, this distance widening slightly for the woods.

The third difference is that you position your hands in front of the ball, and that you choke down slightly on the club, leaving about two inches (5cm) of the grip protruding from the top of your linked hands.

WEIGHT AND POSTURE

Now you are ready to distribute your weight according to the type of shot you are about to play. If you are hitting a pitch from 80 yards (73m) or more to the green, you should favor the left side with about 55 per cent of your weight, and the right with 45

per cent. If the shot is from 35-70 yards (32–64m) out, then the weight is even more toward the left foot, at about 60/40 ratio.

As for posture, that is determined by the club you have selected for the shot. With a sand wedge, for instance, you will be more bent over than if you were using a 9-iron, because the wedge has a shorter shaft. Therefore, you will need to sit back more – or stick out your rear end – to keep your balance throughout the swing, simply because your spine angle is more inclined.

BALL POSITION

Where do you put the ball for a standard pitch shot?

Position it in the middle of your stance or even slightly farther back, depending on how high you want the ball to fly. I explain this further in my other book *Lowering Your Golf Handicap* – along with variations on the standard pitch, such as the lob over a hazard, the low-flying pitch under the wind, and pitching from the rough.

But for the average pitch, setting the ball halfway between the feet is the ideal.

Above and below: When you play the pitch, your weight should favor the left with less weight transfer. This will help you control the shot and get the ball close to your target.

MASTERING THE PITCH SHOT

◆ ◆ ◆ ◆ ◆

Now that I have shown you how to assume the proper set-up for the pitch shot, let's take a look at the basic swing action.

THE TECHNIQUE used for a pitch shot is very similar to the normal golf swing but there is less weight transfer, the back and throughswings are more compact and the emphasis is on accuracy.

Your left hand is one of the keys to the throughswing. This hand must stay ahead of the clubface, then remain ahead of the right hand for as long as possible. At impact, keep your left wrist firm – but not rigid – and focus on striking the back of the ball. It's important not to scoop or chop at the ball as you move forward into a balanced finish.

GAINING FEEL

The standard pitch calls for about a three-quarter backswing, and a follow-through of equal length. But the shorter the pitch, the shorter the backswing and follow-through. That is where 'feel' comes into play and this is a skill that cannot necessarily be taught easily. That's why you must practice this shot

as often as possible to get the hang of it, while also fighting any tendency to decelerate the clubhead at impact.

Try hitting pitches at a variety of distances when you go to the range, picking out a target at 35 yards (32m), then 50 (46m), 70 (64m) and so on – until you can comfortably land the ball to within 'makeable' putting distance. Or set up an open umbrella – upside down, top spike into the ground – in your backyard or garden, and pitch balls into that.

VARYING THE LENGTH

Another key to varying the length of the shot is to narrow your stance slightly for the shortest shots. This naturally cuts down on your turn, while keeping most of your weight on the left side will also help produce the desired effect.

It can also be useful to imagine a clock mounted behind you, and hit different increments on that clockface for each shot.

Placing your hands down the grip is one way of controlling distance on your pitch.

Good tempo is crucial in mastering the pitch. The first move should be low and slow.

Tempo is key

Left: The length of your backswing will be the governing factor as to how far you will hit the ball. When you are practicing these shots, experiment with differing lengths of backswing and note how far the ball travels.

Left: The length of your follow-through should mirror the length of your backswing. This will ensure you don't quit on the shot.

Below: As with all shots, a balanced finish indicates a controlled swing and will help you gain consistency.

For example, a three-quarter swing for a pitch of 85 to 100 yards (78 to 91m) would mean the club stops at about 10 or 11 o'clock on the backswing, and hits the 1 to 2 o'clock mark on the follow-through. A shot of about 50 yards (46m) would mean hitting the 9 o'clock slot on the backswing, and the 3 o'clock mark on the throughswing.

TEMPO IS THE KEY

Even with the shortest pitches, you must be positive or you will commit a multitude of sins. Maintaining a smooth, even tempo is a key factor in the pitch shot. Despite the compactness of the swing, a steady pace is necessary to ensure that the clubhead swings firmly through the ball, just as with any other shot – but perhaps more so with the short irons.

Finally, don't forget what I told you in the sections on preparation and the pre-shot routine. With pitch shots, it's essential to 'visualize' the shot before playing it. Pick a spot on the green and imagine the ball flying through the air, then landing softly, and rolling up to the flagstick.

Now you're ready to hit a solid pitch and shave strokes off your score.

CHIPPING

◆ ◆ ◆ ◆ ◆

What if I guaranteed that you could save six strokes a round by learning just one basic technique? That's right, tomorrow you can finally break 90, 80 or even…well, not so fast. It will not happen tomorrow, because the technique I am now going to explain how to execute – like the pitch – demands a few weeks of practice to learn. But compared to perfecting the full swing, it is easy.

IT'S CALLED chipping, perhaps the most humble – and yet important – stroke in the game. And even though it's often been said that you drive for show and putt for dough, few golfers consistently hit the green in the required one, two, or three strokes regularly to threaten par.

However, as we get better and better, we do get closer to the greens with most shots – and that's where chipping comes into play.

MAXIMUM FEEL

The chip is a stroke played anywhere from a few feet to 30 yards (27m) off the putting surface. The goal is to get the ball close enough with your chip to have a tap-in with your putter on the next shot.

Along the way, you might even hole a few chips, and then that miracle round you have always dreamed about may start to become a very real possibility.

This is another shot that calls for a maximum of 'feel' and imagination. And that means practice, practice…and more practice.

IN A NUTSHELL

Here's how you do it. Any club from a 5-iron to the sand wedge can be used for chipping, depending on the position and lie of the ball relative to the pin, the amount of green you have to work with, and whatever ground you have to carry the ball over to get it rolling on the green. That's the key thing. Get it rolling on the green.

When you're practicing, try rolling the ball underarm toward your target. This will help you visualize the shot rolling toward the hole.

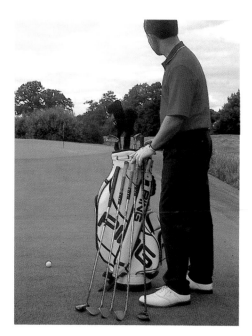

Your first objective is to choose your weapon.

PRO TIP

In recent years, golfers such as Tiger Woods have popularized the idea of using a 3- or 5-wood in certain situations to chip from off the green. Woods uses this club to keep the ball even lower than when chipping with an iron, reducing any risk of a bobble or bounce with the slight initial elevation on a chip shot. The key is to be confident and take an even, smooth stroke.

As Ray Floyd, one of the finest short game players ever and winner of both the US Open and Masters tournaments, said in his book *From 60 Yards In*, this shot 'is simply putting with a lofted club.' Essentially, that's the whole idea in a nutshell, and you'll see why as I describe the technique in these four pages.

JUDGMENT CALL

First, visualize your shot. If you are on the fringe of the green, with say about 30 feet (9m) to the cup, pick a spot where you want the ball to land. Take into consideration the break on the putting surface and any other factors that might come into play – such as the slope or the wind.

The key to executing this shot successfully is your ability to judge distance and how the ball will roll, just as if you were about to hit a putt.

Again, this will take some preliminary practice to get a feel for if you are a beginner, while the more experienced player will have the advantage of being able to conjure up the memory of a similar shot from the past.

But a good rule of thumb is that when you use the standard chipping stroke, and strike the ball with a medium to short iron, the ball will travel about a third of the way to the target in the air and the rest of the way along the ground – depending on the situation.

Conversely if you throw the ball in the air, you inevitably find it more difficult to get the ball close to the hole.

A feel shot

The chip shot can be played from a few feet to up to 30 yards (27m) off the putting surface. When playing the shot, your head should stay very still and your weight should favor the left foot. Feel is the essential factor when playing this shot, and feel can only be developed through practice.

THE BASIC CHIP SHOT

◆ ◆ ◆ ◆ ◆

Now it's time to select your club. Some golfers like to use the same iron for all chip shots, and that's often a pitching wedge or a 7-iron. If you are a beginner, that's probably not a bad idea.

BUT IF you have played the game for a time, you will know that each club produces a slightly different effect, and that club selection is crucial. Picking the right club – in combination with a solid chipping stroke – can make the difference between a long, difficult putt for par versus a short, easy one.

In general, the farther away from the green your ball is lying, the more lofted a club you need to carry the intervening grass or hazard. The added height such clubs naturally put on the flight of the ball will also help impart the backspin needed to check the ball when it hits the green and prevent you shooting past the hole.

ELEVATION AND ROLL

In other words, as I described in the first example above, if you are on the fringe – say only about two to three feet (c.1m) off the green – and the pin is about 30 feet (9m) away, a 6- or 7-iron is ideal, since it will elevate the ball onto the edge of the green, and then let it roll the remaining distance like a well-struck putt.

However, if you are about 15 feet (5m) farther back, you'll probably need a wedge with enough loft to keep the ball in the air about the same distance, and then land the ball on the green and let it roll up to the hole.

Any farther back than that and you would be playing, in effect, a pitch or possibly a lob shot, that may require a different technique.

THE SET-UP

Now you're ready to take your set-up. Position your feet about a foot (30cm) apart in an open stance, angling the front foot out some 20 degrees – just like you did for a pitch – while keeping the rest of your body and the clubhead parallel to the target line. Now concentrate most of your weight on the front foot and position the ball toward the back of your stance, just inside the big toe of your right foot.

Choke down on the club until your lower hand is at the bottom of the grip near the shaft – you can use your putting grip (see Putting) if that feels more comfortable – and push your hands ahead of the ball, so you can hit the shot with a slightly descending contact.

Choke down on the club and ensure that your hands are ahead of the clubhead at address.

Take the club away with the arms and hands.

Regulate the length of swing in relation to the distance of the ball from the target.

Keep your hands ahead of the clubhead and swing through with the back of the left hand moving toward the target.

Setting up a chip shot

Left: Set-up – begin with your normal pre-shot routine: aim the club, align the body, position the ball, grip and posture.

BRUSH OFF

Finally, in order to execute the shot, think about your putting stroke. Keeping your hands, wrists, and arms fairly passive, start the backswing with the same, smooth pendulum motion – arms forming a triangle with the shoulders as the base – that you use for putting.

As you come through the ball, just brush it off the grass, making sure your follow-through is the same length as your abbreviated backswing. And just as you do while putting, keep your head down until the ball is well on its way to the hole.

With any luck, and a solid chipping stroke, by the time you look up, the ball will be disappearing from sight and you'll have a par or birdie on your card.

A putter is a real option when you are close to the green. Remember that the

grass you're putting through should not be too thick and it must be dry.

Right: You will be confronted with many situations where a sand or lob wedge are necessary to lift the ball over a hazard and land the ball softly.

Chipping with a wood

This is the 'Tiger' shot. Played from just off the green, the 3- or 5-wood can be highly

effective in lifting the ball over the apron and rolling the ball toward the hole.

Practice makes perfect.

BUNKER PLAY

◆ ◆ ◆ ◆ ◆

The bunker shot — which strikes terror into most high handicappers — is actually the easiest shot in golf since it leaves the player the highest margin for error.

GREENSIDE BUNKER PLAY

◆ ◆ ◆ ◆ ◆

On most weekends, my golf club is crowded with people using the driving range, playing the course, or enjoying a meal in the restaurant. But the area in front of the clubhouse, where we have a practice bunker and green, is usually deserted – so much so that I often park my car nearby since it gives me easy access to my office.

I KNOW I needn't worry about stray golf balls. Parking there is practically safer than on the street near my own house, since hardly anyone ever uses that bunker. So far, I've yet to suffer a dent, scratch, or smashed window from what would be only a slightly errant shot out of the sand.

MENTAL CAPITULATION

Now why is that? Especially since many golfers are terrified of landing in sand traps, and, once there, are often ready to capitulate mentally. Assuming they will not get up and down for par, they have already resigned themselves to making bogey or worse.

In this section, I'll show you how to gain more confidence when you end up in sand by demonstrating what is really one of the easiest shots in the game. As with any fear or phobia, taking the mystery out of things can go a long way toward solving the problem.

For proof, ask any pro or low handicapper whether he'd rather be in a trap or in the rough, and he will tell you it's no contest. If you're going to make a mistake around the greens – and you will during any round – sand is the best place to find yourself.

From a bunker, you have a large margin of error, you can usually put some spin on the ball, and your chances of getting down in two shots should be better than 50/50.

But like chipping and pitching, practice is the key to mastering this vital shot – although once I convince you of that, I may have to start moving my car to a less convenient parking spot.

Taking the fear out of bunker play comes down to practice. If you fear this shot, read the next few pages and then stay in the bunker until you believe me.

Getting a feel of distance, where you will land the ball, and how the ball will fly is especially important before going into the sand, as often you may be unable to see the flag when playing from a deep bunker.

PREPARATION

The key to playing successfully from the sand is to be positive before you even step into the bunker. How many times have you left the ball in the trap once – or even twice – or bladed it over the other side of the green and into more trouble?

Being afraid of this shot will paralyze your swing and stifle your momentum. And, as with most shots around the green, a smooth but crisp tempo is essential. When a golfer goes into a mini-panic, or is unduly worried, he often fails to swing through the ball, which is the cardinal sin in bunker play. Leaving the clubhead in the sand ensures the ball will stay there as well.

SHOT REHEARSAL

Let's go back to the idea of always rehearsing a difficult shot before hitting it. In the case of bunker shots, this takes on added importance, since this is a unique shot, and it is against the rules of golf to ground your club in the hazard before you take your bunker shot.

First, visualize the shot before getting into the sand – actually conjuring up a mental picture of how the shot works (which I'll explain in a moment) – then imagining the clubhead sliding into the sand, and the ball lifting up on a wedge of sand to the green and trickling toward the hole.

Secondly, I would suggest that you take a few practice swings outside the bunker, using the same set-up and swingpath you will use once inside. When you do go into the bunker, move your feet from side to side to give yourself a firm footing as well as enabling you to assess the depth and texture of the sand.

Now it's time to climb into the bunker and go for that par.

Basics of set-up

Your feet and hips should point left of the target (open stance).

Position your ball on the inside of your left heel.

Keep your weight principally on your left foot throughout your stroke.

THE SAND WEDGE

◆◆◆◆◆

In the 1930s the legendary Gene Sarazen invented the sand wedge, a club that changed the way golf was played. Before that, golfers had to improvize when they found themselves in a bunker, using a variety of clubs in a variety of ways to escape from trouble. So consider yourself lucky to enjoy the benefits of the Squire's creation, and don't neglect to take advantage of it.

THE SAND wedge will always do the job in a bunker if you know how to utilize it, which may seem like an obvious and even labored point. But it isn't. Many golfers never practice this shot. As a result, when they are forced to hit out of sand, they have no idea what this unique club can do, nor how to make it do what Sarazen had in mind – even more than 70 years later!

More surprisingly, some golfers do not even carry a sand wedge in their bags. If you are one of them, remedy that situation immediately – although I would hasten to add that you should first consult with a PGA pro before making a purchase. Choosing a sand wedge with the correct design for the conditions where you play is essential – they do vary.

UP AND OVER

The sand wedge should not to be confused with the pitching wedge, although many beginners tend to mix up the two clubs. With 56 degrees of loft, the sand wedge is designed to lift the ball upward and impart spin, which also makes it handy on the fairway from 80 yards (73m) and less to the green. In addition, there is a wide flange on the sole of this specialized wedge that helps encourage the clubhead to slide through the sand and prevents the leading edge of the blade from digging in – what golf pros refer to as 'bounce.'

I believe the most important aspect of the bunker shot is the follow-through. Too many players stop at impact, so don't get trapped – make a big throughswing taking lots of sand.

Bunker play

That's important because the bunker shot is the only one in golf where we do not strike the ball directly. Instead, the golfer hits one to two inches (2.5 to 5cm) behind the ball, the clubhead passing through the sand and under the ball to lift the ball up and over the forward lip of the bunker and onto the green.

AGGRESSIVE STROKE

Notice I said that the clubhead passes under the ball! In effect, it is the momentum created by a positive stroke that is transferred from the club to sand to the ball. Thus, the sand wedge allows us to hit an attacking shot that imparts spin and stops the ball quickly on the green.

GETTING OUT OF A RUT

A forerunner to Gene Sarazen's modern invention of the sand wedge was a variation on the mid-19th-century club known as a 'cleek' (there were also driving and even putting cleeks), which had a lofted iron blade. Used to play off tight lies and sand, the cleek was ideal for hitting out of cart tracks! In those days, especially along the links land of Scotland, the townspeople had the right of way to cart off sand, gravel, and seaweed, and whatever they could salvage from items routinely washed up on shore from passing ships.

Make your mark – in practice!

When you're practicing (you're not allowed to do this in a game), draw a line in the sand a couple of inches either side of the golf ball. Once you've hit the shot, ensure that all the sand was taken.

But how is it possible to hit aggressively, never touch the ball – and yet get it to travel only a few feet with backspin?

That's where the set-up comes into play. And once you master that, hitting the basic sand shot should become second nature.

Removing sand before the ball is your safety margin that will guarantee success playing from the sand.

The ball is lifted by removing a wedge of sand underneath it

THE BASIC SAND SHOT

◆ ◆ ◆ ◆ ◆

Assume an open stance – with feet, knees, hips, and shoulders angled left of the target line – and with the clubface open to your stance line, but square to the target. The ball should be positioned in the middle of your stance, with the majority of your weight (about 60 per cent) resting on the front foot.

A S WE shall see later, depending on the height you need to achieve to clear the forward lip of the bunker, and the pin placement, these alignments will differ slightly. But, as a general rule, the more height and spin you need, the more you should open your stance and the clubface while also moving the ball farther forward in your stance.

DIGGING IN

Now give yourself a secure, balanced footing by digging your spikes into the sand, twisting your feet until your movement is restricted, the sand about as high as the soles of your shoes. This will also provide more clues about the texture and density of the sand.

With practice and experience, you will learn how to adjust your swing for differing conditions. For instance, with wet, coarse sand, your ball will come out hot and fast, so you may have to shorten your swing. On the other hand, fine, powdery sand will demand

more speed and a longer swing to avoid burying the clubhead. I'll go into more detail about this later.

GRIP AND CHOKE

Now you are ready to grip the club, and although I recommend using your normal grip, some golfers prefer to weaken theirs for a sand shot – to ensure the clubhead stays open. I believe this is a personal preference, but if you normally use a slightly strong grip to help avoid a slice and get more distance, I'd suggest moving to a neutral grip for bunker play to avoid any tendency to dig the clubhead into the sand.

The sand wedge is shaped differently from other clubs in the set as it is made with a flange on the sole to prevent the club digging in.

Far left: Sand wedges do vary in shape, some having a larger flange than others. It pays to hit some different trial sand wedges and find one that suits your game.

Left: Taking your stance in a bunker requires you to dig your feet in. Therefore you need to grip down the club to compensate.

Left: Move your feet in the sand to get a firm footing.

Below left: If you need extra height, open your clubface.

Below: Confidence is the key to good bunker play. Keep your tempo smooth, take sand before the ball, and follow-though.

Bunker play

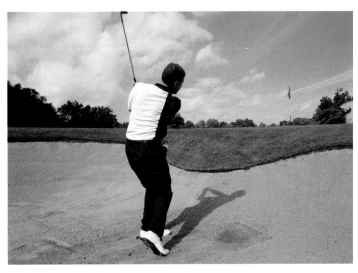

But whatever grip you use, choke down on the club. By twisting your feet into the sand, you have shortened the distance between your hands and the ball, and, as with any shot, you will want to maintain a full extension of your left arm through impact.

POSITIVE HIT

Finally, you're ready to hover the club over a spot on the sand about an inch and a half (4cm) behind the ball, and start your backswing along the line formed by your feet – or along an out-to-in swingpath.

Break your wrists early and take the club back smoothly – good tempo is the key to any bunker shot. As for the length of swing, that will vary with the type of shot required. Consider a three-quarter backswing as about average.

As you begin your throughswing, keep in mind that the crucial element in any bunker shot is not to leave the clubhead in the sand. Hit with a positive blow, slicing through the sand to a full, finished position.

If you do that, I guarantee that the ball will rise high out of the bunker and land softly on the green.

FAIRWAY BUNKERS

◆ ◆ ◆ ◆ ◆

*Fairway bunkers vary from the deep pot bunkers you find on Scottish
links courses, to the generally shallow ones that dot local public facilities.
When you land in a fairway bunker, the first thing you must do is to
assess how high the bank is in front of you, and how close you are to it.*

THEN YOU can decide how prudent
it might be to go for a distance
shot, or just take your medicine and
simply try to get out – using whatever escape
route is open. The first rule with pot bunkers
is to avoid them.

ALMOST INVISIBLE

Generally, they are almost invisible, often
hidden from view when you are standing on
the tee. The land may even slope toward
them, drawing the ball in.

So look at a 'course planner' (a booklet
providing detailed plans of the individual
holes) before you play. Try to establish
where the bunkers are and how far away
they are placed, taking into consideration the
distance you hit a driver or other club off
the tee.

For example, if there is a pot bunker
some 230 yards (210m) from the tee, it
might well be better to use a club that you
can only hit about 215 yards (197m) to
ensure that you cannot reach the sand.

Then you are safe even if you mis-hit the
ball to the left or right of the fairway. For the
average golfer, it just does not make sense to
take on a fairway bunker like the pros do.

If you end up rolling in, you will face a
very tricky second shot.

Where to start

When playing from a
fairway bunker, look at
the top of the ball. Grip
down the club slightly
and consider only a club
that has enough loft to
clear the top of the
bunker.

Above: I'm using a 5-iron as I'm a little farther back in the bunker, compared to the situation below where I'm closer to the bank and so a 7-iron must be used to clear the front lip.

Using a 5-wood

From many fairway bunkers a shallow lip will allow you to hit the shot with anything up to a 5-wood.

Above: Always play a club that you know will get the ball over the front of the bunker.

Left: Even if you have to use a sand wedge, give careful consideration to where you want to play the ball on the fairway for your next shot – you may still make your par.

Using a sand wedge

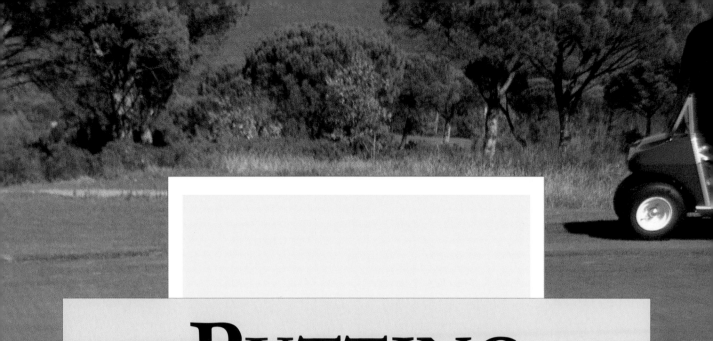

PUTTING

◆ ◆ ◆ ◆ ◆

*Putting accounts for at least
50 per cent of the game, or a
possible 36 strokes taken in an
even-par round of 72.
Here's how to start working
toward cutting your score
dramatically by more
effective putting.*

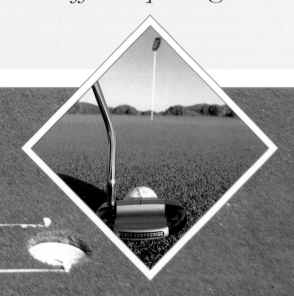

PUTTING

◆ ◆ ◆ ◆ ◆

Drive for show and putt for dough. If a more familiar axiom exists in golf, I don't know what it is. But this one does bear repeating, because like many axioms it contains a crucial element of truth. Putting adds up to 50 per cent of the game, or 36 of the 72 strokes you might take in a round of even par.

PUT ANOTHER way, if you routinely miss just a handful of makeable putts per round, it will mean a major difference to your score and handicap. Instead of playing to an average of around 18 strokes over par, you are in the very mediocre range of the mid-20s duffer. So rather than consistently threatening – or actually scoring – in the 80s, you're struggling to break 100!

VITAL GAME

Does that sound like your game? If it does, then this section is for you – not to mention everyone else who currently plays the game of golf. Name the last player to win a major tournament on any tour on the planet who did not putt well. Or name a great player from any era – from Harry Vardon to Tiger Woods and Colin Montgomerie – who was a poor putter.

Putting is the most vital game within the game of golf, and all the great players are great putters.

CONSISTENT STROKE

Putting well demands a precise physical and mental approach that in some ways is far more demanding than any other shot in golf. As I have stressed in this book, the secret to playing well is having a 'repeatable' swing. The same holds true when you take the putter from the bag.

Simply put, there is little margin for error in this phase of the game. Learning to strike the ball with the same, consistently smooth putting stroke is the only way to start really improving your scores and consistently playing well.

Beyond good mechanics, you also need feel and touch, plus the ability to judge distance. In addition, you must bring that other, less tangible, quality to your putting game that I have also mentioned before – confidence.

NATURAL OUTCOME

The object of every putt is to hole the ball, or at least to leave the next putt within the 'gimme' range. Anything more than two putts on any green is a waste of strokes that will have a significant impact on your scorecard, and may well influence your mood on the next tee with negative consequences.

So let's work first on how to putt more successfully. Once you can do that, the

A consistent, repeatable putting stroke is just as important as a good golf swing. Time devoted to this part of your game will be well rewarded.

natural outcome will be an increase in your confidence. Putt better, and you'll gain confidence. Gain confidence, and you'll putt better. It's a magic circle. In other words, if you approach every putt thinking you can make it, you're halfway there.

Bob Charles – the left-hander whom Jack Nicklaus once called one of the greatest putters ever – said that his putter was the 'life-line' to his game, and the key to every victory he ever achieved – with confidence providing the crucial link between technique and execution.

Remember, the last stroke you take on every hole is a putt, and in many cases – whether it drops in the hole or not – it's often the most significant.

Left: When lifting the ball out of the hole do so at arm's length so as to avoid unnecessary wear around the hole.

Below: One of the reasons that soft spikes are often insisted upon is that metal spikes can cause marks on the green that adversely affect the roll of the ball.

Left: Never up, never in – it's a common saying but so true, Always aim to roll the ball past the hole.

THE PUTTING GRIP

◆ ◆ ◆ ◆ ◆

Golfers use a variety of grips when they putt. Whether pro or amateur, the grips of players I teach are almost as individual as each golfer is. Some use the same grip they employ for the woods and irons – whether the Vardon, interlocking, or ten-finger 'baseball' grip.

OTHERS REVERSE the position of their hands on the club, which is called 'cross-handed' (or 'cack-handed'). A few even putt from the opposite side to the one they use for their normal golf swing. In addition, golfers may choose to set their grip strong, weak or neutral.

COMMON AND SOUND

But the most common grip I see used today is what is called the 'reverse overlap.' It's the one I prefer, and the one I recommend to most golfers I teach. It is the most fundamentally sound putting grip, and offers the average player the highest chance of success. With this grip, the hands are positioned on the club in a way that naturally binds them together as a unit, while removing any tendency to get 'wristy' in the putting motion.

In the reverse overlap, the palms are positioned in opposition to each other, which also provides stability. Combined with the proper set-up and stroke, this grip gives the golfer the best chance of keeping his putter square – or moving it straight along the imaginary target line to propel the ball forward on the correct line to the hole.

ASSUMING A GRIP

Here's how to assume the reverse overlap grip:
• Place your left hand against the grip handle of the putter, leaving a gap at the top of at least an inch (2.5cm). Now grip the club lightly with the middle, third, and little fingers of your left hand. Keeping your forefinger off the shaft, point your thumb straight down the grip.
• Place all four fingers of your right hand on the club, aligning the grip along the pads at the base of the fingers. The little finger of the right hand should be resting snugly against the middle finger of the left hand and the right thumb should also be pointing straight down the grip handle.
• Finally, position your left forefinger in one of the three following ways:
1. Around the little finger of the right hand.
2. Crooked around the ring finger of the right hand – overlapping the last two fingers.

Take time forming your putting grip. Just as in the full swing, the placement of your hands makes a big difference to your final stroke.

The putting grip

Right: The cross-handed grip – the right hand is below the left hand – is worth trying.

Far right: The Langer grip, developed by Bernhard and used to great effect. Only try it if you're desperate!

3. Or run it straight down across all the fingers of the right hand.

Any of the variations described in this final step will form a good reverse overlap grip. Try each one to see which suits you. But remember, only do that when practicing. Never experiment on the golf course!

GRIP PRESSURE

Again, grip pressure is a matter of individual choice.

Tom Watson, one of the best putters ever – even though he's had problems with that aspect of his game in recent years – believes in varying his grip pressure. Watson favors his left hand, so he can guide his stroke with the leading hand. He exerts more grip pressure with the last three fingers of the left hand, plus the index and middle two fingers of the right hand.

Personally I favor keeping the pressure from all the fingers and two thumbs constant throughout the stroke. Hold the club firmly, and yet lightly – much the same way as I recommend you grip both the woods and irons.

FOCUSING GUIDE

When I'm having trouble with my putting, I often try to focus on my left hand for a time, in effect just slightly tightening my grip pressure with that hand in an effort to use it as a guide in stroking the putter toward the hole. I think about keeping it firm throughout the stroke.

Consistency is the key. Experiment with every possible variation in your grip pressure on the practice green. But when putting on the course, make sure you maintain the same pressure throughout the stroke. Any change while playing will distort your feel for the putting motion and may even pull your stroke off-line.

PUTTING YIPS

Some golfers, especially pros and those with more experience, develop the 'putting yips' – a vague, anxiety-related condition that causes a player to stroke across the ball with a short, jerky stab. Often, a golfer can not pinpoint just where or when he or she first developed the problem. But such famous players as Ben Hogan, Tom Watson, and Bernhard Langer have known the agony of suffering through the yips at one or more points during their careers. No absolute cure exists for the yips, because the problem is often psychological and far too complex to analyze. However, overcoming the yips is possible, as both Watson and Langer can attest. The first step to a cure is to experiment with several options, at least for a time. The cross-handed grip – reversing the position of the left and right hand on the putter – that Fred Couples has used is worth trying. A broom-handle putter has also helped Langer and Sam Torrance. Of course, it's impossible to estimate how long someone should adopt a novel approach in trying to overcome the yips. Simply consider any method you choose as a way of getting back to some form of normality and re-gaining confidence. Keep in mind as well that the yips can come from having too much intensity over the ball, much like the idea of 'keeping the head still' during the golf swing. Discipline yourself to take one look and then hit. Spending too much time over the ball causes you to freeze up, and then you will barely be able to move, which can produce a very jagged and irregular stroke. Trust your instincts and try to keep it short and sweet. Finally, when you're practicing before a round, don't hit 20- and 35-foot putts. Instead, hit several short ones. Putting the ball into the hole is the best way to cure the yips, and the yips tend to affect the short putts more than the long ones. Tom Watson has had the most problems with three- to four-foot putts over the past several years, and the greater majority of golfers suffer from the same malaise, finding it easier to deal with a 40-foot putt than a crucial short one.

THE PUTTING SET-UP

◆◆◆◆◆

The putting stance is another area where golfers show how different –
rather than alike – they can be when playing the game of golf. Some set up
slightly open to the ball, while others use a closed stance. Some bend low,
and some stand almost straight up. The arms may be tucked in or flared
out. The feet may be close together or spread wider than shoulder-width.

WHY ALL the differences? Because of two factors common to all putting styles. When putting, every golfer tries to get as comfortable over the ball as possible – which, in turn, ought to breed the confidence needed to make the putt.

Secondly, they are trying to position their eyes directly over or just inside the ball-to-target line.

EYES LINED UP

You can argue the merits of the first case – and I shall in a moment – but there is no disputing the second. Unless your eyes are

lined up above the ball or just inside it, it's extremely difficult to stroke the ball successfully on a line to the hole. In the case of right-handers, this means the left eye specifically.

On the other hand, if your eyes are lined up outside the ball, you will get a distorted view of the target line and will probably pull the putter back on an outside path, which may result in a putt missed to the left.

EVERYTHING SQUARE

So how do you position yourself to make the most putts? I'm all for being comfortable over the ball. But unless you can claim

When I practice my stroke, I choose a flat putt and set up guide lines as shown above.

The putting set-up

Left: Alignment of the clubhead is always rule no. 1 – take time to line up your leading edge.

Opposite left: Now ensure your shoulders, hips, and feet are parallel to your ball-to-target line.

Opposite right: Finally complete putting your hands on the club in your chosen grip.

almost flawless success with your current set-up position – assuming it's somewhat different from the classic one I'm about to explain – try my way for a time.

In watching Bob Charles and Ben Crenshaw over the years – and now Tiger Woods and Jose-Maria Olazabal – I have become convinced that the best putting stances are those where everything is absolutely square to the ball and line of putt – feet, knees, hips, and shoulders.

The ball is forward of mid-stance – or inside the left instep – and the eyes are directly over it, with the arms hanging naturally, forming an almost perfect triangle with the shoulders.

From this position, these pros seem to move the putter effortlessly – first back, and then through the ball – in a rhythmic, pendulum motion. The result? They sink more than their share of putts to capture the big tournaments.

WINNING FORMULA

Here's how to assume that winning formula in your set-up:

• Positioning the ball inside your left heel, set yourself so that your left eye is directly

over the ball. You can test this by dropping a ball down the sight line of your left eye. If you are lined up correctly, that ball will hit the ball on the ground below you.

• Now do try to get comfortable by letting your arms hang naturally, flexing your knees and bending forward from the hips. Wiggle your toes inside your shoes until you balance your weight evenly between both feet – with your feet set at a distance of about 12 inches (30cm) apart.

• Finally, align your body parallel to the line of the putt.

> ### PUTTING IN A STIFF BREEZE
>
> I always widen my stance – and even crouch a bit – when putting in a stiff wind to gain more stability. If you were taking a full swing with this set-up, it would restrict your turn. But since you're putting, you want to minimize any body motion and anchor yourself against swaying off the ball. By the way, don't underestimate the effect of the wind on the line of your putt. A stiff cross-wind can blow a slowly turning putt off-line by several inches. That's why I always recommend that new golfers hire a caddy when playing links courses, where the wind can be especially tricky. A caddy's advice on how a putt will break in the wind can save you several strokes per round.

Above: Your left eye should be directly above the golf ball – if you drop a ball from your left eye, it should land on the ball below.

THE PUTTING STROKE

◆ ◆ ◆ ◆ ◆

The basic putting stroke is like the motion of a pendulum, with the hands, arms, and shoulders moving as one unit. There is no body rotation – the shoulders simply move back and forth. That's why it is important to align yourself correctly at address.

HOWEVER, HERE again many golfers use highly individualistic approaches. Some are very wristy, some jab at the ball, and some even hook it across the target line.

I recommend using the pendulum motion to reduce any variables and take your hands out of the game – which, as we have seen from the driver to the sand wedge, increases the chance of a properly executed shot.

As I have stressed all along, in modern golf the hands serve as a conduit, not as the beginning and end of the swing. The pendulum motion is a long, sweeping action that strokes the ball with topspin toward the hole. Because the hands are passive and work together, the tendency to hit or flick at the ball is greatly reduced.

LOW AND SLOW

Here's how it works. Take the putter back with your hands, arms, and shoulders working together – firmly but without rigidity – the length of the backstroke dictated by the length of the putt.

The clubhead should come back low and slow, just above the ground, and appear to be moving in a straight line – although it will in fact eventually move slightly inside the line on longer swings.

Developing the stroke

Far left: Keep your arms, hands, and shoulders working together. Your putter should be low to the ground – your head must remain very still.

Left: Always accelerate through the ball. Your hands should remain passive throughout – and keep your head still.

Follow the same swingpath into impact – letting the clubhead naturally accelerate from the motion of the swing – until your left shoulder rises slightly and the throughswing is equal in length to the backswing.

The overall feeling should be one of pace, fluidity, and rhythm. Never force the pace, or you'll knock the putt off line. You are stroking through the ball, not hitting it!

ANXIOUS LOOKS

Finally, it is important to realize that many golfers almost complete the putting stroke in fine style, but then look up too quickly, anxious to see how their ball is doing. If you do that, you will miss the putt more often than not. It's like failing to reach a good follow-through position on a shot with a longer club. Injecting a note of anxiety into any golf stroke, especially before completion, will inevitably lead to problems.

Never look up until well after striking the ball. This stops your head from lifting or turning. When you raise your head too soon, or too abruptly, you can cause your shoulders to move and so send your putt off the target line.

As your swing the putter forward, allow the left shoulder to rise slightly – keep smooth and listen for the ball to drop. Remember, don't look up too early.

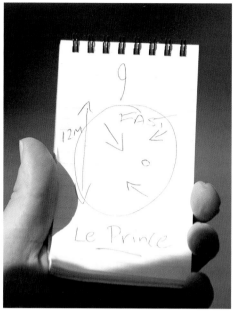

Left: Practice whenever and wherever you get the opportunity – even in the bedroom!

Above: If you have a chance to play a practice round, or you play a course regularly, make some notes about the shape of the green and how the ball rolls.

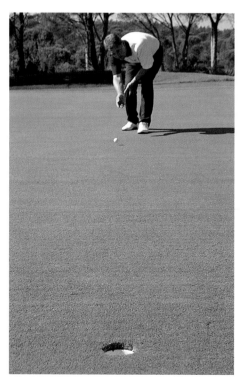

Left: When practicing, roll a ball underarm across the green. It helps you to judge distance and pace more accurately.

Right: Practicing putting to a tee makes the hole on the course look huge.

Right: A miniature slice – the ball will spin right if you swing out-to-in.

Below: Trapping an object between your arms can help to keep arms, hands, and shoulders working together as a unit.

Above: After marking and cleaning the ball, replace the ball with any straight lines parallel to the target line.

Below: Allowing the wrists to flex in the putting stroke is generally disastrous.

PRO TIP

The great American pro Sam Snead had the classic cure for raising your head too soon after the putting stroke. He advised golfers to listen for the sound of the ball plopping into the hole before they looked up! For those who just cannot wait that long, I recommend at least counting to two before allowing your curiosity to get the better of you.

INDEX

◆ ◆ ◆ ◆ ◆